THEORY INTO PRACTICE

Fall 2005 • Volume 44, Number 4

This Issue: Peace Education	275
Essential Components of Peace Education *David W. Johnson and Roger T. Johnson*	280
Lessons to Be Learned From Research on Peace Education in the Context of Intractable Conflict *Haggai Kupermintz and Gavriel Salomon*	293
From Moral Exclusion to Moral Inclusion: Theory for Teaching Peace *Susan Opotow, Janet C. Gerson, and Sarah Woodside*	303
Bringing Peace to the Central City: Forgiveness Education in Milwaukee *Elizabeth A. Gassin, Robert D. Enright, and Jeanette A. Knutson*	319
The Role of Peer Bystanders in School Bullying: Positive Steps Toward Promoting Peaceful Schools *Jodie Lodge and Erica Frydenberg*	329
Conflict, Contact, and Education in Northern Ireland *Ulrike Niens and Ed Cairns*	337
Implementing Community Peace and Safety Networks in South Africa *Tricia S. Jones*	345
School-Based Peace Building in Sierra Leone *Diane Bretherton, Jane Weston, and Vic Zbar*	355
Child Soldiers, Peace Education, and Postconflict Reconstruction for Peace *Michael Wessells*	363
Additional Resources for Classroom Use	370
Index to Volume XLIV	374

Guest Editors: David W. Johnson and Roger T. Johnson

This Issue

THERE ARE TWO MAJOR REASONS why peace education is increasingly of interest for teachers throughout the world. The first is to constructively deal with the aftermath of war and/or the presence of violence in their daily lives. There are countries such as Rwanda, Sierra Leone, Somalia, and Sudan where civil war has motivated educators to try to ensure that the previously warring groups will live together harmoniously. In North America and Europe, the increase in violence and hostile aggression in schools has motivated educators to implement aspects of peace education. In addition, there are immigrant children from war-torn countries who have experienced extreme forms of violence and need to be resocialized into a peaceful, democratic society. In countries such as Australia aspects of peace education are being used to promote reconciliation between the ruling majority and the native peoples who were displaced through colonization. The second is to give students the competencies and values they will need to build and maintain peace in their families, friendship groups, work places, neighbors, countries, and world, as well as within themselves. The building and maintenance of peace on all levels depends on students having certain competencies and values that are primarily taught, practiced, and perfected in the schools. In this issue both of these aspects of peace education are discussed. To place the articles in this issue in context, it is first necessary to discuss the history and nature of peace education and the nature of peace and the ways it is established.

For centuries, peace education was based on the teachings of religious leaders such as Lao Tse, Jesus Christ, Buddha, and Baha'u'Hah, who taught that people were supposed to promote peace in their lives and in the world as a whole. In the middle ages, peace education expanded beyond religion into education (the Czech educator Comenius believed that peace depended on universally shared knowledge) and philosophy (Immanuel Kant believed that peace was achieved through legal and judicial systems). Late in the 19th century, William James wrote an article opposing imperialism and the *war fever*, with which it was associated. In the 20th century, Maria Montessori advocated teaching children to be independent decision makers who would not automatically follow authoritarian rulers urging them to war. Mahatma Gandhi promoted nonviolence as a means to resolve intergroup conflicts. The first academic peace studies program was established in 1948 at Manchester College in Indiana. Peace education gained momentum during the Cold War, when activists worked to prevent nuclear war. The Committee for a Sane Nuclear Policy (SANE) was founded in 1957. In the 1960s, concern about the possibility of nuclear war resulted in modern peace education. Since the 1970s, programs have been initiated at every level of education. Over 300 colleges and universities now have peace studies programs and in many countries elementary and secondary schools have programs that could be described as peace education.

With the proliferation of programs, peace education has become quite diverse and difficult to define. Programs around the world differ widely in terms of ideology, objectives, emphasis, curricula, contents, and practices. Reasons for the diversity include the specific problems the society is trying to solve, the availability of education to citizens, the economic resources available, and the society's political structure. The multitude of definitions of peace education may be grouped into the following:

1. Cognitive definitions, such as learning (a) information about the nature of peace; (b) the philosophies underlying peace, such as nonviolence; (c) international issues such as the United Nations and the proliferation of nuclear weapons, environmental studies, and power and resource inequities; and (d) general subject areas such as social studies, history, and ethnic studies.

2. Affective definitions, focusing on such attitudes and values as optimism, self-regulation, self-efficacy, and commitment to the common good.

3. Behavior definitions, such as the procedures and skills needed to implement the philosophies of nonviolence, build and maintain interdependent systems, and resolve conflicts constructively.

Broadly, *peace education* may be defined as teaching individuals the information, attitudes, values, and behavioral competencies needed to resolve conflicts without violence and build and maintain mutually beneficial, harmonious relationships. The ultimate goal of peace education is for individuals to be able to maintain peace among aspects of themselves (intrapersonal peace), individuals (interpersonal peace), groups (intergroup peace), and countries, societies, and cultures (international peace).

The majority of peace education programs are implemented with no real theoretical or research rationale and are never evaluated. Conceptual frameworks are needed to organize what we know about peace education and guide future program development and research. The primary purpose of this issue of *Theory Into Practice,* therefore, is to make a modest attempt to advance the scholarship in the field of peace education by bringing together into one place some of the more thoughtful, theory-based, evaluated, and successful peace education efforts from all over the world. Johnson and Johnson present programs based on social interdependence, constructive controversy, and integrative negotiation theories; Opotow, Gerson, and Woodside's article is based on moral inclusion theory. The Niens and Cairns, Kupermintz and Salomon, and Wessells articles are based on contact theory; Gassin, Enright, and Knutson discuss forgiveness theory; Jones presents work on mediation theory; and Lodge and Frydenberg's article is based on bystander theory. All articles either present research data or are based on a series of research studies. Together they represent some of the most scholarly union of theory, research, and practice in the field.

To understand the nature and role of peace education, it is first necessary to understand the nature of peace and the ways it is established.

Nature of Peace

Peace is not an easy concept to define. In English, the Latin root word for peace is *pax,* which means a settlement or common understanding that ends or averts hostilities. In Hebrew and Arabic the root word for peace (i.e., *shalom, salaam*) is *shalev,* meaning whole or undivided. In Chinese, peace is written with two characters, one meaning harmony and the other equality or balance; thus, peace is harmony in balance. In Japanese, peace is represented by two characters meaning harmony, simplicity, and quietness. Hindu and Sanskrit have several words for peace (i.e., *avirodha, shanty, chaina*), which mean the absence of war, spiritual or inner peace, and mental peace or calmness. These root words indicate that peace is more than the absence of war, just as health is more than the absence of disease.

Peace may be defined as the absence of war or violence in a mutually beneficial, harmonious relationship among relevant parties (i.e., aspects of a person or among individuals, groups, or countries). This definition indicates that peace may be conceptualized as having two separate dimensions. On the first dimension, war, violence, and strife are at one end (war is a state of open and declared armed combat between entities such as states or nations) and at the other end are settlements, agreements, or common understandings that end or avert hostilities and violence. On this dimension, if war or violence is absent, then peace is assumed to exist. On the second dimension, discordant, hostile interaction aimed at dominance and differential benefit (i.e., winners and losers) and characterized by social injustice is at one end, and mutually beneficial, harmonious interaction aimed at achieving mutual goals and characterized by social justice is at the other end. On this dimension, if the relationship is characterized by positive relationships, mutual benefit, and justice, then peace is assumed to exist.

Peace as a Dynamic, Active, Relationship Process

In defining peace, several aspects of its nature must be taken into account. First, peace is a relationship variable, not a trait. Peace exists among individuals, groups, and nations; it is not a trait or a predisposition in an individual, group, or nation. As a relationship, peace cannot be maintained by separation, isolation, or building barriers between conflicting parties, all of which may temporarily reduce violence (establishing a cold war). Second, peace is a dynamic, not a static, process. The level of peace constantly changes as the relevant parties interact. Peace is not a stable state; it increases or decreases with the actions of each relevant party. Third, peace is not a passive state; it is an active process. Passive coexistence is not a viable path to peace. Building and maintaining peace takes active involvement. Finally, it should be noted that peace is hard to build and easy to destroy. It may take years to build up a stable peace and then one act can destroy it.

Positive Interdependence and Constructive Conflict

Given that peace is a fragile, dynamic relationship among parties that takes active involvement to build and maintain, it should be noted that long-term peace is maintained by mutuality (i.e., positive interdependence). The relevant parties have to commit themselves to achieving mutual goals (commerce, sharing of resources, mutual protection, maintenance of boundaries, etc.), justly distribute mutual benefits, establish a mutual identity, and adopt civic values that include a concern for one another's well-being and the common good. In addition, peace is not the absence of conflict. Conflicts occur continually. Peace is characterized by continuous conflict managed constructively (rather than destructively).

Structural Liberty

Long-term, stable peace is not established by the domination of one party over another. Domination may be direct (through superior military and economic power) or indirect (through structural oppression). Structural oppression is the establishment of social institutions (such as education, religion, and mass media) that create the social, economic, and political conditions (i.e., systematic inequality, injustice, violence, or lack of access to social services) that result in the repression, poor health, or death of certain individuals or groups in a society. Long-term, stable peace requires structural liberty where social institutions promote equality, justice, and the well-being of all relevant parties.

Intractable Conflicts

Peace is most challenging (and peace education is most needed) in intractable conflicts. Examples include the conflicts in Northern Ireland, the former Yugoslavia, the Israeli–Palestinian conflict, and the conflict between Turkish and Greek citizens in Cyprus. These are conflicts in unavoidable relationships that are difficult to resolve, intense, and ongoing, each side viewing their own group as righteous and their opponents as evil. They are intergroup conflicts with a history of severe imbalances of power between the parties characterized by domination and perceived injustice. The current high-power group tends to exploit, control, and abuse the other group while promoting legitimizing myths about their superiority. Some intractable conflicts persist for centuries, being institutionalized and transferred from generation to generation. The hope of resolving such conflicts is peace education.

Most of the articles in this issue deal with peace education in countries marked by intractable conflicts. Kupermintz and Salomon present a series of studies involving Israeli and Palestinian participants in peace education programs. Jones describes a study of school and community based mediation programs in South Africa. Gassin, Enright, and Knutson discuss a program in teaching forgiveness to intercity minority children in the United States. Niens and Cairns describe studies of structured contact between Catholic and Protestant students in Northern Ireland. Bretherton, Weston, and Zbar, as well as Wessells, describe different peace education programs (one involving the schools and one focused on the community) in Sierra Leone. All of these articles describe important and often courageous work in war-torn countries.

Ways to Establish Peace

To understand the purpose of peace education, it is helpful to review the three ways of establishing peace: (a) Peacekeeping separates the disputants and/or provides incentives to stop fighting to end ongoing violence, hopefully without resorting to violence in the process. Peacekeeping may suppress violence but does not resolve underlying grievances. (b) Peacemaking creates (through such processes as negotiation, mediation, and arbitration) a resolution of the conflict, a cease-fire, or a framework for resolving the conflict in the future. Peacemaking may resolve the immediate conflict but often fails to deal with underlying issues that may reignite the conflict in the future. (c) Peacebuilding creates the economic, political, and educational institutions needed to ensure long-term peace based on social justice. Doing so removes the structural bases of oppression and destruction conflict and establishes new (or modified) structures that create the processes necessary for social justice and peaceful relations among former disputants. An example is ending a totalitarian government and establishing a democracy that guarantees equal justice for all. The articles in this issue all deal with peacebuilding.

Conclusions

Peace may be defined as the absence of war or violence in a mutually beneficial, harmonious relationship among relevant parties. Peace education, therefore, may be defined as teaching individuals the information, attitudes, values, and behavioral competencies needed to resolve conflicts without violence and to build and maintain mutually beneficial, harmonious relationships. Peace is dynamic (not static), a relationship (not a trait), and an active process (not a passive state). It is based on mutuality (positive interdependence) and the constructive management of conflict. Long-term peace depends on structural liberty. The greatest challenge for peace is in intractable conflicts, which often last for centuries. With the dramatic increase in world interdependence, peace education has become prominent everywhere. The breadth and scope of peace education is far too broad to include here. Most of the programs being implemented, however, are divorced from relevant social science theory and research. The contributors to this issue represent some of the most thoughtful and effective social scientists involved in peace education. They have done landmark work in many areas of the world where it is quite challenging and even dangerous. It is our hope that bringing these articles together will help guide and stimulate the field. Certainly, the prevention and mitigation of war and the building and maintenance of peace depends on efforts similar to those reported in this issue. And where is a better place to begin then with the children who occupy a nation's schools?

Guest Editors
David W. Johnson
Roger T. Johnson

David W. Johnson
Roger T. Johnson

Essential Components of Peace Education

Peace education is a key for establishing a consensual peace and maintaining it over time. There are 5 essential elements in building a lasting peace through education. First, a public education system must be established that has compulsory attendance for all children and youth, integrated so students from previously conflicting groups interact with one another and have the opportunity to build positive relationships with each other. Second, a sense of mutuality and common fate needs to be established that highlights mutual goals, the just distribution of benefits from achieving the goals, and a common identity. In schools, this is primarily done through the use of cooperative learning. Third, students must be taught the constructive controversy procedure to ensure they know how to make difficult decisions and engage in political discourse. Fourth, students must be taught how to engage in integrative negotiations and peer mediation to resolve their conflicts with each other constructively. Finally, civic values must be inculcated that focus students on the long-term common good of society.

David W. Johnson and Roger T. Johnson are Professors of Educational Psychology at the University of Minnesota.
Correspondence should be addressed to David W. Johnson, Educational Psychology, University of Minnesota, 60 Peik Hall, 158 Pillsbury Drive S.E., Minneapolis, MN 55455. E-mail: dwj@visi.com

TO DISCUSS THE ESSENTIAL components of peace education, it is necessary to understand peace and peace education and discuss the two ways of establishing peace, imposed peace and consensual peace. We present an overall plan for peace education, emphasizing teaching students the competencies and values they need to build and maintain peace on a consensual basis. These include building and maintaining cooperative systems, making decisions about the difficult issues involved in maintaining peace, and resolving conflicts among the relevant parties in constructive ways, all of which inculcate the civic values needed to maintain peace. These essential elements need to be built into the ongoing, day-to-day fabric of school life so students get years of training in how to nurture a peaceful society. Peace education needs to be powerful enough to make a difference even in intractable conflicts.

Ways of Establishing Peace

Ways of establishing and maintaining peace may be classified on a dimension with imposed peace at one end and consensual peace at the other end (Clark, 2001).

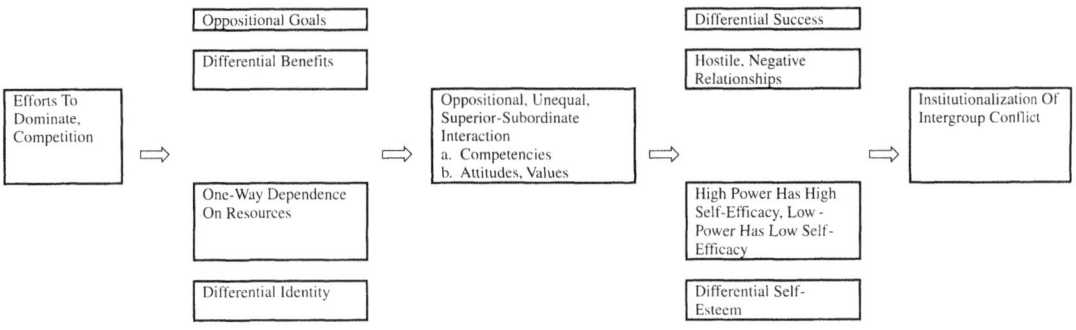

Figure 1 Imposed peace.

Imposed Peace

Imposed peace is based on domination, power, imposition, and enforcement. High-power groups use their military and economic power to force low-power groups to end hostilities and implement the peace accords (see Figure 1). There are two ways in which peace may be imposed: By the winners in a conflict or by powerful third parties such as the United Nations, NATO, or other international alliances. In both cases, military or economic power is used to ensure hostilities are ended. However, imposing peace suppresses the conflict but does not resolve underlying grievances and does not establish positive long-term relationships among disputants.

Peacekeeping: Third party imposes peace. Powerful third parties may impose peace on disputants through the exercise of military or economic power. Peacekeeping involves suppressing violence by separating disputants and/or providing incentives for disputants to stop fighting. Examples include a police force that separates two rival street gangs to end a street war or an international military force that keeps two conflict groups separated from each other. The third party separates the disputants and ensures that contact between disputants is limited and controlled. The advantage of peacekeeping is that it ends a violent, destructive behavior in a conflict. Peacekeepers are supposed to behave as a neutral third party who will not take sides. If peacekeepers are seen as taking sides or as acting in oppressive and abusive ways, then the conflict may be transferred to them and disputants may then act violently toward the peacekeepers or at least attempt to obstruct the effectiveness of the peacekeeping. Peacekeeping does not, however, end the conflict and may in fact create a new conflict between the disputants and the peacekeepers. This is especially likely if the peacekeepers act in oppressive and abusive ways toward the disputants.

The goal of peacekeepers is to end violent behavior by separating disputants. The goal of the disputants is to win by dominating or decimating the opposing groups. Though there are advantages to having the violence ended, the basic conflict among the disputants is not resolved and the actions of the peacemakers basically obstruct the goal achievement of the disputants.

Domination: Winner imposes peace. When one group wins a war or gains significant military or economic advantage over the other disputants, the high-power party may use its advantage to dominate the low-power groups and impose peace on the high-power group's terms. The goal of each group is to win and, when one does, the other groups lose. When the winner imposes peace, the losing groups are often segregated or assigned specific areas where they are to live. Contact between the groups may be limited and controlled.

Long-term maintenance of peace is attempted through structural oppression (i.e., ensuring social institutions such as education, religion, mass media, and political structures all promote the status quo of the high-power group's domination and privilege). Peace education may focus on institutionalizing the status quo through the indoctrination of low-power citizens in the importance of accepting the domination of the high-power citizens as the natural order of the world, as God's will, or as in their best interests. Members of the high-power group are taught a complementary rationale for their privileged position (God has appointed them rulers, nature made them genetically superior, etc.). Such institutionalization typically fails, as the imbalance of power tends to result in oppression and injustice, creating rejection of the status quo by the low-power groups and leading to continued conflict.

Negative interdependence. The imposition of peace often has destructive effects, perhaps best explained through social interdependence theory (Deutsch, 1962; Johnson & Johnson, 1989). When peace is imposed, negative interdependence exists among parties; that is, there is a negative correlation among parties' goal achievements: One party may obtain its goals if and only if the other parties involved fail to achieve their goals. In addition to oppositional goals, negative interdependence may exist through differential distribution of benefits (winners receive more benefits than losers) and a one-way dependence on resources (i.e., low-power parties are dependent on the resources of high-power parties, but not vice versa). The identities of the parties are differentiated in that members of the high-power group have a positive self-concept as a winner and members of the low-power groups have a negative identity based on being losers. The disputing groups will tend to perceive each other as unequals (i.e., winners and losers). This is based on a unidimensional view of each other taking into account only the characteristic most salient for winning or losing (military or economic power, history of privilege, or cultural or tribal background; Johnson & Johnson, 1989).

Negative interdependence tends to result in oppositional or contrient interaction. Parties attempt to obstruct others' efforts to achieve their goals. The obstruction of each other's efforts to achieve the goal is characterized by a lack of *substitutability* (i.e., the actions of one party do not substitute for the actions of another), *negative cathexis* (i.e., the investment of negative psychological energy toward the actions of the peacekeepers or opposing group and the groups themselves), and *negative inducibility* (i.e., resistance to being influenced by the peacekeepers or the opposing group; Deutsch, 1962).

The negative interdependence characterizing relationship between the party imposing peace and the parties on whom peace is being imposed tends to result in the dominant group gaining a higher share of the benefits than the subordinate groups, negative and hostile relationships among the groups involved, and differential psychological and physical well-being (i.e., high power parties have high self-efficacy and self-esteem whereas low-power parties have low self-efficacy and self-esteem along with stress related illnesses).

Consensual Peace

The consensual approach to peace is based on reaching an agreement that (a) ends violence and hostilities and (b) establishes a new relationship based on harmonious interaction aimed at achieving mutual goals, justly distributing mutual benefits, being mutually dependent on each other's resources, and establishing a mutual identity (see Figure 2). In consensual peace, all parties believe

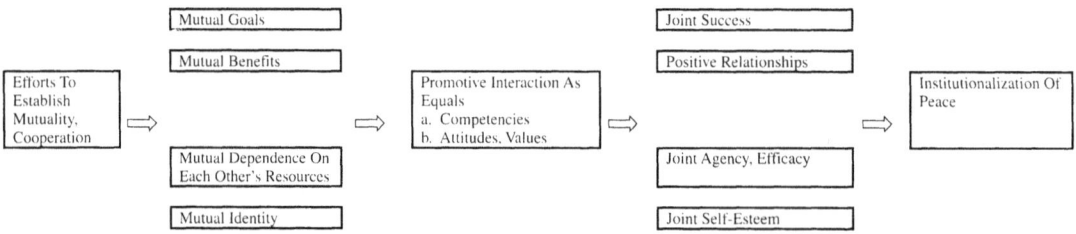

Figure 2   Consensual peace.

that peace is desirable, legitimate, just, and beneficial. Because all parties have a fair chance to influence the decision, their commitment to implement the decision is maximized and they are obligated to abide by the agreement and promote each other's efforts to do so (although a small minority within each party can sabotage the agreement by violating it). The result is a joint success in maintaining the peace, positive relationships among the involved parties, a sense of joint agency and efficacy, and joint self-esteem. The foundation on which consensual peace is built is positive interdependence.

There are two levels of consensual peace. The first level is *peacemaking*, in which the parties involved negotiate a cease-fire, an initial agreement, or a framework for resolving the conflict in the future. Peacemaking typically manages the immediate conflict but fails to deal with underlying structural issues. The second level is *peacebuilding*, in which the economic, political, and educational institutions are used to create long-term peace. Peacebuilding deals with the structural issues and is aimed at creating long-term harmonious relationships based on mutual respect and social justice. Peace education is one means of institutionalizing consensual peace. Peace education may focus on building mutuality among all citizens and teaching them the competencies, attitudes, and values needed to build and maintain cooperative systems, resolve conflicts constructively, and adopt values promotive of peace.

Positive interdependence. Consensual peace is perhaps best explained through social interdependence theory (Deutsch, 1962; Johnson & Johnson, 1989). When peace is consensual, it is based on mutuality or positive interdependence. Positive interdependence exists when there is a positive correlation among individuals' goal attainments; one party can achieve its goal if and only if all other relevant parties achieve their goals (Deutsch, 1962; Johnson & Johnson, 1989). Examples of such goals are trade agreements or economic alliances, clarification of boundaries, mutual defense, or environmental preservation or cleanup. Though peace depends on such mutual goals, positive interdependence may be strengthened through the just distribution of mutual benefits, dependence on each other's resources, and the development of a mutual identity that subsumes all relevant parties into one superordinate group (such as North American as well as Canadian, American, and Mexican). Generally, parties involved in a cooperative effort perceive each other as equals. This does not mean that their resources are identical or that each will contribute the same amount of resources in every situation. Rather, it is based on a multidimensional view of others that recognizes that, in the long-run, over a variety of situations, each party will contribute approximately equally to the overall success of the joint efforts (Johnson & Johnson, 1989).

Positive interdependence tends to result in promotive interaction. The promotion of each other's efforts to achieve the goal is characterized by *substitutability* (i.e., the actions of one party substitute for the actions of another), *positive cathexis* (i.e., the investment of positive psychological energy in the actions of the other groups and the other groups themselves), and *positive inducibility* (i.e., openness to being influenced) (Deutsch, 1962).

The outcomes of the promotive interaction may be classified into three categories. The first is joint success in achieving the mutual goals and distributing the benefits in an equable and just manner. The second is building positive and supportive relationships among the diverse parties. The third is psychological and physical well being, which includes a sense of joint agency–efficacy and joint self-esteem. Joint efficacy is the shared belief by collaborators in their collective power to achieve a goal, solve a problem, or accomplish a task (Bandura, 2000; Johnson & Johnson, 1985, 1989, 2003). Individuals have to work together to achieve goals they cannot accomplish on their own. Joint self-esteem is a judgment about joint self-worth, the combined competence or value of all parties. It is possible, for example, for males or females to have a gender self-esteem inclusive of all members of the category, or for Canadians to have a joint self-esteem inclusive of all citizens of that country.

Institutionalizing Consensual Peace Through Peace Education

The steps of institutionalizing consensual peace through education include (a) establishing public education that is compulsory and integrates the diverse members of society, (b) establishing the mutuality and positive interdependence underlying a peaceful society and teaching students the competencies and attitudes they need to engage in cooperative efforts, (c) teaching students how to engage in peaceful political discourse to make difficult decisions, (d) teaching students how to engage in integrative negotiations and mediation, and (e) inculcating civic values.

Step One: Establishing Public Education

Mandating compulsory education. For peace education to influence children and youth, they must attend school. A necessary condition for accomplishing the goals of peace education is, therefore, the existence of mandatory public education. There are many reasons why a national education system is needed. First, education gives children and youth hope for a rewarding and meaningful livelihood and life. The lack of educational opportunities is a major motivator to join terrorist and rebel groups in many countries. Thus, establishing a public education system is necessary to prevent continuing warfare. Second, private school systems, such as those formed by religious groups, often exploit children and youth's idealism and commitment to religion, sense of victimization and social injustice, and disaffection with society to teach pro-war ideology and socialize children and youth into beliefs that justify violence as a means of obtaining political and religious goals. Third, schools provide the means to reintegrate children and youth who have participated in violence back into civilian life and help them find meaningful and positive roles as civilians. Education is needed to reestablish normal societal life in countries trying to end violent conflicts.

Fourth, schools provide a setting where peace may be lived and experienced, not just talked about. To experience peace, schools need to be integrated (discussed later) and school life needs to reflect the mutuality, cooperation, political discourse and decision making, and constructive conflict resolution inherent in a peaceful society. Peace is woven into the fabric of school life primarily through instructional methods. It is reflected in the ways lessons are taught, student–student and student–teacher conflicts are managed, decisions are made, and intellectual conflicts are resolved. The meaning and relevance of peace education arises out of students' day-to-day personal experiences in building and maintaining peace in the school.

Fifth, schools provide the setting where students may be educated in the competencies and attitudes they need to build and maintain long-term peace, not just information about peace. The social resources (i.e., individuals skilled in being part of a cooperative effort, making difficult decisions, and resolving conflicts constructively) needed for peace to flourish are developed through experiencing the processes of building and maintaining peace in their day-to-day life in the school. Because the competencies and values every student should master for peace to be established and maintained take years to master, their use should pervade classroom life from elementary through postsecondary education.

Integrating schools. For peace to be developed, positive relations must be established among members of formerly disputing groups. Segregated schools have cultural and social consequences. Students are introduced into opposing cultural worlds through the curriculum tailored for their cultural group. Socially, the very separation of different groups emphasizes the differences and hostilities. Students are thus culturally and socially taught the values, attitudes, norms, and information underlying the continuation of the conflict. The more different the groups are in terms of culture, religion, ethnicity, history, and so on, the more destructive the effects of segregation may tend to be. Peace tends to be very fragile in segregated societies and long-term peace is at risk.

Integrating schools, however, has to be more than the simple idea that proximity would resolve intergroup conflict. Just putting people in contact with one another does not in and of itself resolve the conflict, and contact can even make the situation worse. Contact under certain conditions can increase intergroup hostility, whereas under other conditions it can create positive relationships among members of disputing groups. Thus, contact is a necessary but not sufficient condition for decreasing prejudice and intergroup hostility. The conditions under which contact will reduce intergroup hostilities and build positive relationships among diverse people are (a) working together cooperatively to achieve common goals (no competition between groups), (b) interaction on a personal level where candid conversations may take place, (c) equal status, and (d) support for the contact from authority and group norms (Allport, 1954; Johnson & Johnson, 1989). In an extensive meta-analysis of the research on intergroup contact, Pettigrew and Tropp (2000) concluded that optimal intergroup contact was a key aspect of any successful effort to reduce prejudice and that the effects on prejudice reduction are much stronger when contact is conducted in work and organizational settings such as schools rather than travel and tourism settings.

For long-term consensual peace to be established and maintained, therefore, the students from all relevant groups must interact and build positive relationships. Integrating schools provides the opportunity for diverse students to interact and get to know each other. The more different the groups in terms of culture, religion, and so forth, the greater the need for integration. Though this may seem almost impossible in many countries, it is a goal that should be worked toward.

Step Two: Establishing Mutuality, Positive Interdependence

Establishing positive interdependence. Peacebuilding requires that mutuality to be established on three levels: mutual goals, mutual benefits from achieving goals (i.e., common fate), and mutual identity. These three types of positive interdependence need to be institutionalized in the economic, political, and educational institutions of the society. Long-term peace depends on having common goals that unite all members of a society in a joint effort. The mutual goals have to be salient and compelling enough to overcome competing agendas, the past history of conflict among the parties, and the dynamics of intergroup conflict (Johnson & Lewicki, 1969; Sherif, 1966). The benefits received from achieving the mutual goals must be justly distributed among all relevant parties. Usually, benefits need to be equally distributed, although in some cases those with the most need may be given more than others. Equal benefits tend to highlight the common fate of all members of the society. Mutuality is also established through a superordinate identity that makes all citizens members of the same group. This mutual identity is created by (a) respecting one's own cultural identity, (b) respecting others' cultural identities, (c) developing a superordinate identity that subsumes all the diverse identities, and (d) basing the superordinate identity on a pluralistic set of values. The United States provides an example, where Norwegian Americans, Swedish Americans, African Americans, Hispanic Americans, and others are all united by being American. Such levels of identity may be extended from one's family, community, or tribe to the country as a whole, to the region in which the country exists, and eventually to the world as a whole. For consensual peace to flourish, all parties need to be united by a superordinate identity.

Correspondingly, all sources of negative interdependence and isolation must be eliminated. Competition among the formerly disputing groups for economic resources, political power, and educational achievement will institutionalize the conflict and encourage further violence. As long as the disputants are isolated from each other, continued conflict may be institutionalized.

Using pedagogy to build a cooperative community. Peace education is concerned with fostering schools where students work together to achieve mutual goals, distribute the benefits justly, and develop a superordinate identity that unites all students in the school. The easiest way of doing so is through the use of cooperative learning (Johnson, Johnson, & Holubec, 1998a, 1998b). *Cooperative learning* is the instructional use of small groups so students work together to maximize their own and each other's learning. There are three types of cooperative learning. *Formal cooperative learning* consists of students working together, for one class period or several weeks, to achieve shared learning goals and complete specific tasks and assignments (such as decision making or problem solving, completing a curriculum unit, writing a report, conducting a survey or experiment, etc.). *Informal cooperative learning* consists of having students work together to achieve a joint learning goal in temporary, ad-hoc groups that last from a few minutes to one class period. Informal cooperative learning groups are often organized so that students engage in 3- to 5-min focused discussions before and after a lecture and 2- to 3-min turn-to-your-partner discussions interspersed throughout a lecture. *Cooperative base groups* are long-term, heterogeneous cooperative learning groups with stable membership. Base groups give the support, help, encouragement, and assistance each member needs to make academic progress (attend class, complete all assignments, learn) and develop cognitively and socially. Base groups are permanent (lasting from one semester or more) and provide the long-term, caring peer relationships necessary to influence members consistently to work hard in school.

In addition to experiencing cooperation in learning groups, the classroom and school may be structured into a cooperative community—a group of people who share the same locality, goals, and culture. *Classroom interdependence* may be created through such procedures as class goals, rewards, roles (e.g., establishing a class government), or dividing resources (e.g., a class newsletter with an article from each group). *Interclass interdependence* may be created through organizing several classes into a neighborhood and having joint projects. *School interdependence* may be structured through displaying the school's goals, organizing faculty into collegial teaching teams and study groups, using cooperative groups during faculty meetings, and conducting all-school projects. Projects with parents, such as creating a strategic plan or raising money, create *school–parent interdependence*. Finally, *school–neighborhood interdependence* may be created by mutual projects, such as having neighborhood members play in the school band or having students and neighborhood members jointly clean up a park. Through these layers of interdependence, schools can promote peace within the community as well as among students.

Cooperation is most effective when it is structured to contain five basic elements (Johnson & Johnson, 1989). First, there must be a strong sense of positive interdependence, so individuals believe they are linked with others so they cannot succeed unless the others do (and vice versa). Second, each collaborator must be individually accountable to do his or her fair share of the work. Third, collaborators must have the opportunity to promote each other's success by helping, assisting, supporting, encouraging, and praising each other's efforts to achieve. Fourth, working together cooperatively requires interpersonal and small-group skills, such as leadership, decision making, trust building, communication, and conflict management skills. Finally, cooperative groups must engage in group processing, which exists when group members discuss how well they are achieving their goals and maintaining effective working relationships.

Through experiencing cooperative learning in all subject areas and grade levels, students gain a cognitive understanding of the nature of cooperation and mutuality, procedural competencies of how to initiate and maintain cooperative efforts, and the emotional commitment to attitudes and values underlying cooperation and mutuality (e.g., valuing the well-being of collaborators and oneself, promoting the common good).

It is within cooperative learning groups that the personal relationships and emotional support are developed that allow for candid conversations about the conflict previous to the peace agreement. These candid conversations involve the honest and detailed sharing of past experiences, pain, and insights involved in the healing of past traumas. Even in extreme, seemingly intractable conflicts, such candid conversations allow for reconciliation, forgiveness, and the giving up of an identity as a combatant or victim.

Achieving mutual goals and establishing a joint identity requires that members of the diverse groups interact with each other and promote each other's success. Through promoting each other's success and building positive relationships with each other, students become more sophisticated about their differences and engage in candid discussions concerning their relationships. The personal relationships and candid discussions are critical, as it takes more than superficial connections to overcome stereotyping and prejudice and to build an inclusive caring that extends to all parties relevant to the peace.

Step Three: Teaching Students How to Make Difficult Decisions

Maintaining peace requires that hard decisions are made by members of the diverse groups in ways that ensure all citizens are committed to implement the decision. Peace education includes (a) facing the difficult issues that must be discussed for peace to be established and maintained, (b) establishing a procedure that all parties agree to use to discuss these issues, (c) training students how to use the procedure skillfully, and (d) incorporating the use of the procedure into students' personal identity and value system so the procedure will be habitually used. When left unresolved, the difficult issues may result in a renewal of war or violence. To have constructive discussions of these issues, the parties involved need an effective decision-making procedure. A procedure that provides a model of the political discussions inherent in democracy and can be used in academic teaching is *constructive controversy*.

A controversy exists when one person's ideas, opinions, information, theories, or conclusions are incompatible with those of another and the two seek to reach an agreement (Johnson & Johnson, 1995). Controversies are resolved by engaging in what Aristotle called *deliberate discourse* (the discussion of the advantages and disadvantages of proposed actions) and are aimed at synthesizing novel solutions (i.e., creative problem solving). Teaching students how to engage in a controversy begins with randomly assigning students to heterogeneous cooperative learning groups of four members. Each group is divided into two pairs and given an issue on which to write a report and pass a test. One pair is given the *con* position on the issue and the other pair is given the *pro* position. The cooperative goals of reaching a consensus (by synthesizing the best reasoning from both sides), writing a quality group report, and ensuring all members pass the test, are highlighted. Students then

1. Research, learn, and prepare position: Students prepare the best case possible for their assigned position by researching the assigned position, organizing the information into a persuasive argument, and planning how to advocate the assigned position effectively.

2. Present and advocate position: Students present the best case for their assigned position to ensure it gets a fair and complete hearing and listen carefully to the opposing position. The intent is to persuade others to agree with them.

3. Engage in an open discussion in which there is spirited disagreement: Students freely exchange information and ideas while (a) arguing forcefully and persuasively for their position, (b) critically analyzing and refuting the opposing position, and (c) rebutting attacks on their position and presenting counter arguments.

4. Reverse perspectives: Students reverse perspectives and present the best case for the opposing position.

5. Synthesize: Students drop all advocacy and find a synthesis on which all members can agree. They summarize the best evidence and reasoning from both sides and integrate it into a joint position that is a new and unique. Students write a group report detailing the synthesis and its supporting rationale, and take a test on both positions. Members then process how well the group functioned and celebrate their success and hard work.

Such intellectual *disputed passages* (compared to debate, concurrence-seeking, and individualistic efforts) create higher achievement, longer retention, more frequent use of higher level reasoning and metacognitive thought, more critical thinking, greater creativity, and continuing motivation to learn (Johnson & Johnson, 1989, 1995). In addition, more positive interpersonal relationships develop and participants' self-esteem and liking for the experience improve. The effective discussion of difficult issues, furthermore, promotes the development of moral courage and the ability to face opposition and argue against other points of view. It enhances the willingness to speak out and act in support of important values in the face of opposition.

Step Four: Teaching Students How to Resolve Conflicts Constructively

If peace is to last, individuals must learn how to resolve conflicts constructively. In many countries, schools may include students who only know violent methods of settling disputes. To build peace, all students need to know how to resolve conflicts in constructive and nonviolent ways. Though peacemaking may involve distributive (win–lose) negotiations, peacebuilding requires the use of integrative negotiations, where disputants strive to find a resolution that maximizes the benefits for all parties rather than determining who wins and who loses. Working together cooperatively, and resolving conflicts constructively, sets the stage for reconciliation and forgiveness. In building and maintaining peace there are usually difficult conflicts that take great skill on the part of all parties to resolve. Resolving such conflicts constructively requires the use of integrative negotiations. Students learn such procedures as part of peace education. The conflict resolution program that has the most research validation is the *Teaching Students To Be Peacemakers Program.*

The Teaching Students To Be Peacemakers Program began in the 1960s to teach all students how to resolve conflicts of interests constructively by engaging in problem-solving negotiations and peer mediation (Johnson & Johnson, 1996a, 2005). A conflict of interests exists when the actions of one person (attempting to maximize his or her wants and benefits) prevent, block, or interfere with another person maximizing his or her wants and benefits. Conflicts of interests are resolved through negotiation and mediation. There are two types of negotiations: *distributive* or *win–lose* (where one person benefits only if the opponent agrees to make a concession) and *integrative* or *problem solving* (where disputants work together to create an agreement that benefits everyone involved). In ongoing relationships, distributive negotiations result in destructive outcomes, and problem solving leads to constructive outcomes. The steps in using problem solving negotiations are (Johnson & Johnson, 2005) as follows:

1. Describing what you want. "*I want to use the book now.*" This includes using good communication skills and defining the conflict as a small and specific mutual problem.
2. Describing how you feel. "*I'm irritated.*" Disputants must understand how they feel and communicate it openly and clearly.
3. Describing the reasons for your wants and feelings. "*If I don't get to use the book soon my report will not be done on time. It's frustrating to have to wait so long.*" This includes expressing cooperative intentions, listening carefully, separating interests from positions, and differentiating before trying to integrate the two sets of interests.
4. Taking the other's perspective and summarizing your understanding of what the other person wants, how the other person feels, and the reasons underlying both. "*My understanding of you is ...*" This includes understanding the perspective of the opposing disputant and being able to see the problem from both perspectives simultaneously.
5. Inventing three optional plans to resolve the conflict that maximize joint benefits. "*Plan A is ... , Plan B is ... , Plan C is ...*" This includes inventing creative options to solve the problem.
6. Choosing one and formalizing the agreement with a hand shake. "*Let's agree on Plan B!*" A wise agreement is fair to all disputants and is based on principles. It maximizes joint benefits and strengthens disputants' ability to work together cooperatively and resolve conflicts constructively in the future. It specifies how each disputant should act in the future and how the agreement will be reviewed and renegotiated if it does not work.

A mediator is a neutral person who helps two or more people resolve their conflict, usually by negotiating an integrative agreement. In contrast, arbitration is the submission of a dispute to a disinterested third party (such as a teacher or principal) who makes a final and binding judgment as to how the conflict will be resolved. Peer mediation consists of four steps (Johnson & Johnson, 2005):

1. Ending hostilities: Hostile encounters are broken up and students are cooled off.
2. Ensuring disputants are committed to the mediation process: The mediator introduces the process of mediation and sets the ground rules that (a) mediation is voluntary; (b) the mediator is neutral; (c) each person will have the chance to state his or her view of the conflict without interruption; and (d) each person agrees to solve the problem with no name calling or interrupting, being as honest as he or she can, abiding by any agreement made, and keeping anything said in mediation confidential.
3. Helping disputants successfully negotiate with each other: The disputants are carefully taken through the problem-solving negotiation steps.
4. Formalizing the agreement: The agreement is solidified into a contract.

The role of mediator is rotated so all students serve as mediators an equal amount of time. Initially, students mediate in pairs. This ensures that shy or nonverbal students get the same amount of experience as more extroverted and verbally fluent students. Teaching all students to mediate properly results in a schoolwide discipline program where students are empowered to regulate and control their own and their classmates' actions. Teachers and administrators are then freed to spend more of their energies on instruction.

The Peacemaker Program has been implemented from kindergarten through high school (Johnson & Johnson, 1996a, 2005). It results in students and faculty learning the negotiation and mediation procedures, retaining their knowledge throughout the school year and into the following year, applying the procedures in conflicts, transferring the procedures to nonclassroom settings such as the playground and lunchroom, transferring the procedures to nonschool settings such as the home, and (when given the option) engaging in problem solving rather than win–lose negotiations.

When integrated into academic units, the Peacemaker Program increased academic achievement and long-term retention of the academic material. Academic units, especially in subject areas such as literature and history, provide a setting to understand conflicts, practice how to resolve them, and use them to gain insight into the material being studied. The program also resulted in students developing more positive attitudes toward conflict. Students viewed conflicts as potentially positive and faculty and parents perceived the conflict training as constructive and helpful. Finally, students tended to resolve their conflicts without the involvement of faculty and administrators and, consequently, the number of discipline problems teachers had to deal with decreased by about 60% and referrals to administrators dropped about 90%.

It should be noted that conflicts cannot be resolved constructively when they occur in competitive and individualistic conditions. In a competitive context, individuals strive to win rather than solve the problem. In an individualistic context, individuals tend to care only about their own self-interests and ignore the interests of others. It is only in a cooperative context that conflicts are resolved constructively.

Step Five: Inculcating Civic Values

Consensual peace is maintained through the application of civic values. Peace survives on the virtue of the people and virtue is reflected in the way individuals and groups balance their own needs with the needs of the society as a whole. Motivation to be virtuous is created by a sense of belonging to an inclusive society, a concern for the society as a whole, and a moral bond with the society whose life is at stake. When parties work together to achieve mutual goals and when conflicts are managed constructively within decision-making and conflict-of-interests situations, the adoption of the civic values underlying civic virtue is promoted (Johnson & Johnson, 1996b, 2000). The inculcation of these values should be encouraged and nurtured. For consensual peace to exist and be sustained, the relevant parties must share common values aimed at equality and justice. To create the mutuality that defines a peaceful relationship, there must be shared values that define appropriate behavior. Mutuality cannot exist in settings dominated by competitive or individualistic efforts. Rather, students need to internalize the values reflective of cooperation, controversy, and integrative negotiations, which include commitment to the common good and to the well being of others, a sense of responsibility to contribute one's fair share of the work, respect for the efforts and viewpoints of others and for them as people, behaving with integrity, empathy with and caring for the other parties, compassion when other members are in need, equality, and appreciation of diversity. Such civic values underlie and are promoted by the cooperation, controversy, and constructive conflict resolution that take place in the school. In addition to promoting consensual peace, individuals who hold these values tend to lead happier and healthier lives.

Cooperation, Controversy, and Integrative Conflicts as Automatic Habit Patterns

Every cooperative learning lesson is also a lesson in social skills and how to organize and conduct cooperative efforts. Every controversy lesson is also a lesson in political discourse and decision making. Every integrative negotiation and mediation lesson is also a lesson in seeking creative resolutions of conflicts that allow all parties involved to reach their goals while maintaining effective working relationships. Cooperative learning, constructive controversy, and the Peacemaker Program are designed to be used with all students at all grade levels, becoming more complex and sophisticated each year. As the procedures are used regularly in academic units, students practice and learn to use them in nonthreatening academic situations. It takes considerable practice to master the cooperation, controversy, and peacemaker procedures at a level where they are automatically used without conscious thought or planning. Throughout the school year, therefore, teachers should structure almost all lessons cooperatively and integrate the controversy and peacemaking procedures into academic lessons (e.g., in studying *King Lear*, students can role play each conflict using the integrative negotiation and mediation pro-

cedures). Teachers should also conduct specific skill lessons on communication skills, controlling anger, appropriate assertiveness, problem solving, perspective taking, creative thinking, and a wide variety of other related interpersonal and small-group skills (Johnson, 2006; Johnson & F. Johnson, 2006). Short-term peace education programs tend to have short-term effects; it takes a long-term program to have long-term effects. Once they are in students' behavioral repertoire, the cooperation, constructive controversy, and peacemaking procedures can be used in the societal situations that determine whether peace continues or ends.

Conclusions

Peace may be imposed (either by the most powerful party in the conflict or by powerful third parties who provide peacekeepers) or may be based on a consensual agreement about goals, benefits, and the sharing of resources. Once established, peace is institutionalized through the economic system, political structures, education, religion, housing patterns, and mass media. There are five essential elements in institutionalizing peace through education. First, for education to influence children and youth, compulsory public education must be established. To build the long-term positive relationships needed to institutionalize peace, the schools must be integrated so the children and youth from the disputing groups interact with each other, get to know each other, and build positive relationships. This contact must occur under optimal conditions (i.e., working together cooperatively, building personal relationships in which candid conversations may take place, equal status, support from authorities, and societal norms).

Second, mutuality and an awareness of a common fate must be established so individuals perceive that the goals of any one group can be accomplished if and only if the goals of all other groups are accomplished. The benefits of achieving the mutual goals must be distributed in a just and fair manner. A superordinate identity unifying the diverse groups must be built. There are a variety of ways to teach mutuality, but the most effective may be to use cooperative learning to ensure that mutuality is built into the day-to-day fabric of school life. The school becomes a microcosm of society by having students work together cooperatively to achieve mutual learning goals. The pedagogical procedures weave mutuality into the fabric of school life and can be extended to cooperative classrooms and an overall cooperative school structure.

Third, the children and youth in many societies have never lived in a democracy and are unfamiliar with the role of a citizen in a democracy. Dissent may have been punished. They need to learn, therefore, how to engage in democratic decision making involving political discourse. This may be taught through the constructive controversy procedure. Mastery of the democratic decision-making procedures may be achieved through the frequent use of the constructive controversy procedure to teach academic material.

Fourth, many of the children and youth attending school may have participated in the conflict as warriors, support personnel, or victims. They are used to seeing violence as the primarily strategy for dealing with conflicts. They need, therefore, to learn how to manage conflicts constructively. To teach students how to resolve conflicts of interests constructively, the Peacemaker Program (consisting of integrative negotiation and peer mediation procedures) needs to be implemented at all grade levels. The conflict procedures need to be integrated into the curriculum.

Finally, the civic values necessary for consensual peace need to be inculcated, such as commitment to the common good and to the well being of others, a sense of responsibility to contribute one's fair share of the work, equality, and compassion when other members are in need. By engaging in cooperative efforts, making difficult decisions, and resolving conflicts constructively, students will internalize these values.

These five steps need to be implemented at all levels of schooling so students from formerly adversarial groups experience positive interaction for years and the cooperative, controversy, and conflict resolution procedures become automatic habit patterns and the underlying values become firmly embedded. The personal experiences resulting from cooperation and constructive conflict resolution among diverse students result in an understanding of the meaning and relevance of peace and justice and define a way of life. It also institutionalizes peace in educational settings.

References

Allport, G. (1954). *The nature of prejudice.* Reading, MA: Addison-Wesley.

Bandura, A. (2000). Exercise of human agency through collective efficacy. *Current directions in psychological science, 9*(3), 75–78.

Clark, I. (2001). *The post-cold war order: The spoils of peace.* Oxford, England: Oxford University Press.

Deutsch, M. (1962). Cooperation and trust: Some theoretical notes. In M. R. Jones (Ed.), *Nebraska symposium on motivation* (pp. 275–319). Lincoln: University of Nebraska Press.

Johnson, D. W. (2006). *Reaching out: Interpersonal effectiveness and self-actualization* (9th ed.). Boston: Allyn & Bacon.

Johnson D. W., & Johnson, F. (2006). *Joining together: Group theory and group skills* (9th ed.). Boston: Allyn & Bacon.

Johnson, D. W., & Johnson, R. (1985). Motivational processes in cooperative, competitive, and individualistic learning situations. In C. Ames & R. Ames (Eds.), *Attitudes and attitude change in special education: Its theory and practice* (pp. 249–286). New York: Academic.

Johnson, D. W., & Johnson, R. (1989). *Cooperation and competition: Theory and research.* Edina, MN: Interaction Book Company.

Johnson, D. W., & Johnson, R. (1995). *Creative controversy: Intellectual challenge in the classroom* (3rd ed.). Edina, MN: Interaction Book Company.

Johnson, D. W., & Johnson, R. (1996a). Conflict resolution and peer mediation programs in elementary and secondary schools: A review of the research. *Review of Educational Research, 66,* 459–506.

Johnson, D. W., & Johnson, R. (1996b). Cooperative learning and traditional American values. *NASSP Bulletin, 80*(579), 11–18.

Johnson, D. W., & Johnson, R. (2000). Cooperative learning, values, and culturally plural classrooms. In M. Leicester, C. Modgil, & S. Modgil (Eds.), *Values, the classroom, and cultural diversity* (pp. 15–28). London: Cassell PLC.

Johnson, D. W., & Johnson, R. (2003). Student motivation in cooperative groups: Social interdependence theory. In R. Gillies & A. Ashman (Eds.), *Cooperative learning: The social and intellectual outcomes of learning in groups* (pp. 136–176). New York: RoutledgeFalmer.

Johnson, D. W., & Johnson, R. (2005). *Teaching students to be peacemakers* (4th ed.). Edina, MN: Interaction Book Company.

Johnson, D. W., Johnson, R., & Holubec, E. (1998a). *Cooperation in the classroom* (6th ed.). Edina, MN: Interaction Book Company.

Johnson, D. W., Johnson, R., & Holubec, E. (1998b). *Advanced cooperative learning* (3rd ed.). Edina, MN: Interaction Book Company.

Johnson, D. W., & Lewicki, R. (1969). The initiation of superordinate goals. *Journal of Applied Behavioral Science, 5,* 9–24.

Pettigrew, T., & Tropp, L. (2000). Does intergroup contact reduce prejudice?: Recent meta-analytic findings. In S. Oskamp (Ed.), *Reducing prejudice and discrimination* (pp. 93–114). Mahwah, NJ: Lawrence Erlbaum Associates, Inc.

Sherif, M. (1966). *In common predicament.* Boston: Houghton-Mifflin.

Haggai Kupermintz
Gavriel Salomon

Lessons to Be Learned From Research on Peace Education in the Context of Intractable Conflict

Recent research on peace education entails important practical lessons about educational work in regions of intractable conflict. Peace education in this context must deal with collective narratives and deeply rooted historical memories and societal beliefs. Research findings from a series of studies with Israeli and Palestinian students and teachers demonstrate the challenges of attaining durable and worthwhile effects through educational activities: short-term benefits may erode over time, ongoing violence and hostility may block attempts to understand the opponent's perspective, and power and status asymmetries may dictate incompatible agendas or prohibit a mutual common ground for constructive interaction. At the same time, these studies offer several promising directions to enhance the potential of carefully designed peace education programs. Such programs are likely to foster participants' ability to acknowledge the adversary's collective narrative, engage in constructive negotiations over issues of national identity, and express a less monolithic outlook of the conflict.

Haggai Kupermintz is an Assistant Professor and Codirector of the Center for Research on Peace Education at the University of Haifa. Gavriel Salomon is a Professor and the Director of the Center for Research on Peace Education at the University of Haifa.
Correspondence should be directed to Haggai Kupermintz, Center for Research on Peace Education, University of Haifa, Haifa, 31905, Israel. E-mail: kuperh@construct.haifa.ac.il

ONE OF THE JUSTIFICATIONS for carrying out research on peace education programs is the nontrivial lessons that can be derived from them to design and improve future peace education practices. We focus here on the practical lessons that can be learned from recent research on peace education in the context of an intractable conflict. Such a conflict is characterized by being violent, perceived as a zero sum game (where one gains only if the other loses), irreconcilable, central, and total in a society's life (Rouhana & Bar-Tal, 1998). We wish to claim that peace education in such regions differs in important ways from regions with nonviolent intergroup tension based on ethnocentrism (Bar-Tal, 2004), or in regions of relative tranquility, such as Sweden, as well as from education for interpersonal conflict resolution as conceptualized and practiced in schools (Salomon, 2002).

There are at least three qualities that set aside peace education in regions of intractable, often bloody, conflicts that distinguish it from other programs. First, the main focus of peace education in areas such as Northern Ireland, Kosovo, Israel/Palestine, or Rwanda, is not the conflict between individuals who need to acquire conflict resolution skills but rather between collectives (Coleman, 2003). As individuals, members of groups involved in the conflict may not directly engage in actual conflict resolution. Indeed, there is no conflict to be skillfully resolved between an individual Hutu and an individual Tutsy in Rwanda (Staub, 2002), or between Israelis and Palestinians as particular individuals. The focus of peace education in such conflicts is on the treatment of the collective conflict (Azar, 1990; Foster, 1999), rather than the acquisition of particular skills for interpersonal conflict resolution (Deutsch, 1993; Sandy, Bailey, & Sloane-Akwara, 2000).

Second, intractable conflicts are deeply rooted in each side's collective narrative, the story each side tells about itself, its identity, aspirations, perceived role in the conflict, and, mainly, its past and current history (Bruner, 1990; Salomon, 2004). History, in particular, holds the conflicting sides in a firm grip that often ignites and then sustains the continuation of the conflict (Devine-Wright, 2001; Roe & Cairns, 2003). Think of the way memories of the 14th Century Turkish conquest of Kosovo played out 600 years later in the conflict between Albanians and Serbs (Troebst, 1998), or the role that the collective memory of the *Naqba* (catastrophe) of 1948 play for the Palestinians in their fight against the Israelis (Tamari, 2002). This is one of the major challenges facing peace education in the context of such conflicts; it is a challenge not often faced by peace education in either a region with no adversaries or in situations requiring conflict resolution in schools.

Third, peace education in the context of intractable conflicts faces the challenge of deeply rooted beliefs held by each side about itself (we are right, God is on our side, we are the victims) and about the adversary (they are wrong; they are the aggressors; they understand only the language of force; they force us to do ugly things; Bar-Tal, 2000). Such collective beliefs are perceived as unquestioned truths and are thus highly resistant to change (Weick, 2001).

Conflict resolution programs in schools do not face similar challenges of collective narratives, histories, and beliefs (though they may encounter weak manifestations of such issues). Their main concern is with the cultivation of orienting, perception, emotional communicational and creative abilities, the creation of positive and supportive classroom environments, as well as the development of conflict resolution skills (Bodine & Crawford, 1998). It is for this reason that much of the research carried on in such programs is of only partial relevance for peace education in the context of intractable conflict; peace education in Northern Ireland would be far more concerned with intergroup mutual understanding (Cairns & Hewstone, 2002). Still, there is partial overlap between the different kinds of peace education and conflict resolution, commonly aiming at the improvement of understanding the nature of conflict, listening, and empathy. Thus, some of the lessons described later, although derived from research in a country of violent and protracted conflict, may be partly applicable to programs in contexts of tranquility or school-based programs of conflict resolution.

In what follows we report on a few studies conducted on peace education programs with Israeli-Jews and Palestinians and point out some general lessons that we have learned from them. These lessons are applicable beyond the context in which the studies were carried out. We have chosen studies where difficulties or failures were encountered as well as more successful ones, as both kinds of studies are very instructive.

No Lasting Change Without Continued Scaffolding

The use of dialogue or encounter groups is typical of peace education programs in the context of interethnic, national, or religious conflict. Youngsters of both sides meet for weekend seminars, concentrated workshops, theater groups, summer camps, and other forms of face-to-face encounters. These encounters are often based on the contact hypothesis—actual face-to-face meeting and the attempt to attain a common goal can challenge and change participants' hostile views of each other. Much research has been carried out on such groups and lists of conditions to be met have been formulated (Pettigrew, 1998). When the conditions are met, friendships between members of the two groups often emerge during participation in the structured encounter activities. But do they generalize to other members of the groups who are not present at the encounters? Research conducted in relatively peaceful contexts appears to provide a positive answer (Pettigrew, 1997). However, research in Cyprus with groups of Greek and Turkish Cypriots, based on the Fulbright Training Program, failed to find a pattern of friendship generalization (Angelica, 1999).

Bar-Natan (2005) conducted a study with 172 Jewish Israeli and Palestinian youngsters who participated in a 3-day intensive encounter group in the village-like retreat of Givat Haviva. She gathered reports of evolving friendships and measured changes in willingness to associate with other members of the opposite group (Social Distance) and willingness to legitimate the collective narrative of the other side. Positive changes were observed at the end of the workshop on both measures, statistically associated with the emergence of friendships between Jews and Palestinians. The results lend limited support to the hypothesis that interpersonal friendships generalize, at least as reflected in a reduction of declared social distance between the groups. It appears that evolving friendships can facilitate a more general acceptance of the other side and its collective narrative. But when the same measures were taken 6 months later, all of the positive changes appeared to have vanished. Levels of social distance and acceptance retreated to where they were before the workshop started; moreover, no associations with the friendships that emerged 6 months earlier were found. In other words, the workshop appears to have left no trace 6 months after it was completed.

Though errors of measurement and poor validity of the measures might account for some of the disappointing results, it is reasonable to hypothesize that changes in perceptions and attitudes attained following a short peace education intervention cannot remain intact over time without consistent and repeated scaffolding. Two factors play an important role here: time and adverse political events. Though still-unstable friendships between members of the adversary groups may have evolved during the workshop, they could not have been sustained without continued contact and maintenance. The attraction of continued contact, in the absence of face-to-face meetings, has a tendency to erode (Hewstone & Brown, 1986). In addition, the ongoing violence on both sides of the divide can easily and adversely affect one's willingness to remain in contact with a member of the enemy group even through remote means such as e-mail or phone calls.

It follows quite clearly that if positive effects are to be attained and sustained over time, and in the face of eroding forces, hit-and-run, shot-in-the-arm-like interventions cannot suffice. Repeating face-to-face meetings or, in other cases, repeatedly reinforcing other critical program elements becomes a necessity. A similar conclusion has been reached regarding Northern Ireland's curricula of mutual understanding (Kilpatrick & Leitch, 2004). Such a conclusion is not unique to peace education in contexts of intractable conflicts, as research on conflict resolution in the schools demonstrates (Sandy et al., 2000). However, the need for continuous intervention, with ongoing reinforcements of the changes attained, is particularly important where those changes are under constant threat of being nullified by ongoing violence and the hatred that accompanies it, as well as by the general belligerent social atmosphere that opposes such changes (Bar-Tal, 2002).

In light of the aforementioned, one may question the validity of attitudinal or behavioral changes recorded *only* at the immediate conclusion of a program, as is often the case. For example, Liebkind and McAlister (1999) introduced high school students to texts and peers modeling tolerance towards foreigners. Though the two-session class intervention had the desired effect on tolerance, as measured by self-reports, there is reason to suspect that the recorded changes may have been short lived. Such changes are in danger of disappearing in the absence of a continued intervention.

The Value of Studying a Distant Conflict

One of the goals often formulated for peace education is to study the conflict and the positions of the other side. Indeed, coming to grips with the adversary's perspective, trying to step into its shoes, legitimizing its narrative and identity (Salomon, 2002), and developing some empathy for its plight (e.g., Bar-On, 2000) are important goals for peace education. However, intuition and experience suggest that, in the context of an intractable conflict, presenting the other side's perspective is most likely to arouse strong resistance. This is the case because one of the effects of an intractable conflict is the development of a tunnel vision (Rapoport, 1974), resulting in what Kruglanski (2004) labeled *epistemic rigidity*: strong adherence to one's narrative and position, and rejection of information that threatens collectively held beliefs. How can such rigidity and resistance be overcome?

Lustig (2002) studied the effects of a program that included the study of a totally foreign conflict. Sixty-eight 12th-grade Israeli-Jewish students studied the Northern Ireland conflict for a few weeks. Not a word was said about the local Israeli–Palestinian conflict, although it is very likely that the analogy between the two conflicts did not escape students' attention. Indeed, this is precisely what Lustig set out to study: To what extent did the program participants transfer their conclusions about the Northern Ireland conflict to their local context of conflict? To what extent were they able to take their adversary's perspective once they came to understand the two-sidedness of the remote conflict they had studied?

Findings were surprising. When asked to write an essay explaining the conflict from the Jewish point of view, program participants and nonparticipants (control group) had no difficulty showing that their own group's collective narrative of the conflict is familiar to them. However, when then asked to write about the conflict from the Palestinian point of view, most of the program participants wrote well-balanced and impartial essays but only a handful of the nonparticipants wrote anything at all. Moreover, analyses of the essays in terms of first and third figure writing, proportion of negative to positive expressions, length, and so on, showed that the Palestinian essays written by program participants did not differ from their Israeli essays. Not so with the few and very short Palestinian essays written by the nonparticipants, which were filled with negative expressions using mainly the third figure when describing the Palestinian perspective. It became evident that where the program participants appeared to be able to step into the Palestinian shoes, those who did not participate in the program were unable to do the same.

This is where theory and research pertaining to transfer of learning becomes applicable: Something learned in an emotionally neutral context was spontaneously transferred to another, emotionally loaded, context. A new understanding of the adversary's perspective emerged, as manifested in the participants' ability to assume the *other's* point of view and present it in a nondefensive and balanced manner. It appears that the study of the foreign conflict afforded the opportunity to engage in a process of rising to a bird's eye view of the two-sidedness of a conflict, then applying the constructed abstraction to the local conflict. The feared resistance was thus circumvented by allowing the students to approach the emotionally loaded local conflict from a more universal, possibly more abstract perspective (Perkins & Salomon, 1992).

Strong Negative Emotions Can Undermine the Best of Intentions

Another suggestion to acquaint students with the collective narrative of an adversary is through induced compliance, that is, inducing each side to present the narrative of the *other* side. This approach is based on the veteran social psychological theory of dissonance reduction, in which a discrepancy is created between the presentation of the other side's perspective and one's (less than positive) attitude toward it. To make the presentation and attitude congruent, people tend to change their attitudes to become more in line with the narrative as they have just presented it. That change is also assumed to be reinforced by the new information that one discovers while presenting the other side's narrative. It would seem that designing a program in which each side prepares and presents in as honest, balanced, and fair a way as possible the point of view of the other side, should lead to desirable changes. The narrative of the other side would now seem less rejectable to those who presented it. Indeed, research inspired by this idea tends to support the feasibility of the approach (Leippe & Eisenstadt, 1994). However, the research so far has not been carried out in the context of a severe, intractable conflict. Would it work also in such a context?

Ayelet Roth (2005) involved two pairs of Jewish-Israeli and two pairs of Israeli-Palestinian teachers in an Internet-based exchange of perspectives. Jewish teachers were to write the Palestinian narrative and the Palestinian teachers the Israeli one. The participating teachers were volunteers who were strongly motivated to cooperate with the other side. They were also knowledgeable of the narratives as construed by each side, so absence of relevant knowledge was not an obstacle.

Roth's study took place during a very difficult time. The days were filled with intensive acts of aggression—the height of the Palestinian uprising and the peak of the Israeli military incursion into Palestinian towns. Numerous individuals were hurt and a general atmosphere of uncompromising belligerence and hatred dominated the media and the political arena. Feelings were raw and very intense. Israeli-Palestinians felt that their brethren in the Palestinian Authority were viciously attacked whereas the Israeli-Jews felt threatened by terror attacks.

The study participants expressed similar feelings in no uncertain terms in their Internet exchanges and during interviews that followed. Little wonder, therefore, that the process of induced compliance never got off the ground. Neither side succeeded in writing the narrative from the other's point of view. Instead, Internet messages, decreasing in numbers as time passed, included expressions of anger, frustration, despair, and defensive expositions of one's own opinion on the ongoing events. Expressing strong views of the violent situation and blaming the other side for its actions dominated the exchanges.

Does this mean that induced compliance cannot serve peace education? Not necessarily. It appears that one's ability to change perspectives and examine the conflict from the opponent's point of view depends on a willingness to step out of one's own traditional role and assume the opponent's position (Leippe & Eisenstadt, 1994). It also depends on confidence of the individual that, in assuming the other's position, one's own stance or identity does not become threatened. However, the presence of an ongoing, violent conflict heightens negative emotions and makes people stick more stubbornly and defensively to their shared perspectives (Bar-Tal & Salomon, in press; Coleman, 2003; Rapoport, 1974), preventing them from engaging in the delicate process of induced compliance. As the study participants reported during interviews, they felt they needed to defend their position and found it impossible to abandon it and role-play that of their opponent.

Heightened emotionality interferes with the more rational process of assuming the other's position. Furthermore, strong negative emotions, such as anxiety and anger, interfere with cognitive performance in general (Mikulincer & Nizan, 1988; Sarason, 1975), and with attempts to change attitudes in particular (Eagly & Chaiken, 1993). Intervention methods that may be relatively effective in unemotional situations and with emotionally neutral targets of change may not be effective with heightened emotionality. It follows that, before any steps are taken to change attitudes or behaviors related to the other side of a conflict, neutralizing negative feelings as much as possible would be helpful.

How can this be attained? Based on the accumulation of experience and research, Maoz and Bar-On (2002) recommend the *To Reflect and Trust* (TRT) approach, where participants share their personal stories and experiences. Given two approaches to dialogue and encounter groups—the interpersonal where the conflict is disregarded in favor of promoting a warm interpersonal atmosphere, and the collective identity approach of confrontation and identity building (Suleiman, 2004)—the TRT takes the middle road. It allows participants to share and reflect on their personal experiences, rooted as they are in the collective narrative, while at the same time promoting interpersonal relations, empathy, and trust (Bar-On & Kassem, 2004). It appears that this approach has the potential to take the sting out of the heightened negative feelings and allow processes such as perspective taking and induced compliance to take place.

Asymmetry of Needs, Perceptions, and Outcomes

Intractable conflicts are marked by sharp asymmetries of power and status between the rivaling parties. The dimensions of inequality can encompass access, opportunities, and mobility to economic, military, civic, and cultural resources. Moreover, in many intractable conflicts the two parties are at different stages of their ethnic, national, political, or cultural growth trajectories; it is common to find an emerging national entity that struggles for independence against a well-established nation-state (as are the cases of the Israeli–Palestinian, the Turkish–Kurdish, or the Spanish–Basque conflicts). Consequently, the material and psychological needs and expectations of the two sides are unique and distinct, and the socially constructed meaning of key concepts of justice, responsibility, or reconciliation would be expected to reflect such asymmetries. These concepts are, in turn, interwoven into the fabric of collective narratives (Bruner, 1990) that embody each community's shared identity and provide a sense of meaning and coherence to the community. Peace education programs that seek to promote contact and dialogue between members of the adversary societies must negotiate powerful and robust differences in core identity elements that may prohibit establishing even a tentative mutual understanding of key concepts that serve as a common ground for constructive interaction.

Biton (2002) studied the differences in Israeli and Palestinian youth's perceptions of the concept of peace and the impact of peace education on these perceptions. The study employed Galtung's (1969) conceptual distinctions among *negative* peace (the absence of violence), *positive* peace (cooperation, harmony, commerce, and mutuality), and *structural* peace (equality, independence, and sovereignty).

About 300 Jewish-Israeli and Palestinian youth (aged 15–16) participated in a year-long in-school educational program, designed by the Israel–Palestinian Center for Research and Information (IPCRI). The program seeks to promote self-awareness, understanding, and tolerance for others in one's immediate surrounding, and to cultivate acceptance of the *distant others*—members of the adversary society. Before participation in the program, 87% of the Jewish-Israeli students stressed the negative aspects of peace whereas 89% Palestinians stressed its structural aspects, as reflected in responses to structured questionnaires, free associations, explanations, perceived utility, and suggested strategies to attain peace.

Such different conceptions reflect the discrepancies in both side's needs, aspirations, and basic interpretations of events and issues. Moreover, these differences show the lack of agreement on the seemingly mutually desirable outcome of peace. The Jewish-Israeli concern with security and the Palestinian desire for independence are incompatible aspirations. Any attempt to reconcile these two competing demands through education must first bring them to light and weigh their importance for understanding participants' attitudes, expectations, and goals. Anticipating a generalized perceptual or attitudinal change in response to a peace education program runs the risk of neglecting the necessary adjustments needed to optimize the program to its participants.

When prompted again at the end of the peace education program, 37% (up from about 10%) of the Jewish-Israeli group and 26% (up from 5%) of the Palestinian group stressed the positive aspects of peace, compared with a control group which did not show any change over time. Still, Jewish-Israeli students continued to put more emphasis on the negative meaning of peace, but at the same time showed a dramatic increase in their perceptions of the structural elements of peace.

The role of competing agendas in shaping processes and outcomes of structured intergroup encounters in educational settings is exemplified in a study of curricular cooperation of Jewish and Palestinian teachers in Israel (Maoz, 2000). Inspired by Sherif's (1966) Robber's Cave experimental demonstration of the potential of joint activities to help improve intergroup relations, peace education programs sought to incorporate structured encounters where members of adversary societies engaged in joint projects. Typically, these encounters were studied from a perspective of attitude change but less attention was devoted to the intergroup processes during the encounters. Some researchers forcefully argued that, in a context of intractable ethnonational conflict, the power and status asymmetries between the sides inevitably penetrate the dynamics of encounters (Rouhana, 1997; Suleiman, 2004).

In Maoz's study, teams of Israeli Jewish and Palestinian teachers were convened to work together over 1 school year and create study units on Jewish and Arab affairs to be implemented later in their respective schools. Only 6 of the 15 teams managed to produce a study unit, and of these only two teams got to teach the units in their classrooms. The analysis of the group dynamics during work sessions revealed that the seemingly neutral, equal-status setting became a stage where the intricacies of the external intergroup conflict were played out vigorously. The joint pedagogical work was often devalued in favor of discussing the Jewish–Arab conflict, although such discussions were officially restricted by program organizers. In particular, the Palestinian teachers wanted to discuss the past and the harm which, in their eyes, was done to them by the Israelis. The Israeli teachers tried their best to avoid such discussions and wanted, instead, to concentrate on the meetings' tasks—to write curricular units. There was hardly a common agenda for the meetings.

These patterns of incongruent, even conflicting agendas underscore the need for a better understanding of the set of expectations, aspirations, and interpretations with which peace education participants enter the educational experience. Theory and practice of instructional design have long acknowledged the importance of recognizing and incorporating individual and group differences in planning and implementing learning experiences. Peace education will be well advised to adopt a similar view. We wish to argue that programs that are better attuned to the unique sensitivities each party brings to the learning situation stand a better chance of clarifying important concerns and familiarizing each side with the perspectives of the other, hence affording a less monolithic outlook on the conflict.

But this is not the only lesson to be learned from the Maoz study. A second lesson pertains to the possibility of unexpected outcomes of intergroup encounters. Group dynamics in that study were characterized by the formation of subgroups and collations—crossing national lines and splintering the group of impartial third-party organizers and facilitators—around particular disputes that arose over the issue of setting the agenda for the task-team encounters. The legitimacy of exposing the political conflict during the meetings became a topic around which participants formed a microcosm of the larger conflict.

The ability to experience and work through painful issues during their joint work led many teachers to express satisfaction with the encounters, although most of them failed to achieve the prescribed goal. It appears that learning the perspectives of the other side was a major, although not anticipated, outcome of a type of cooperation between participants that arose naturally in the groups. The product of this cooperation was not the official task designated by the organizers, but rather the processing of pressing issues that reflected the different needs and aspirations of the two groups. The conflict was not pacified by the joint work on the pedagogical project; however, the experience of cooperation did provide a framework in which key issues of national identity and the demand for recognition could be negotiated, if not resolved. It might well be that the unanticipated encounter with conflict-related issues, previously avoided, was a goal worth attaining.

Summary

Our purpose in this article was to draw a number of lessons from recent research on peace education in a region of intractable and violent conflict with the hope that these lessons could inform program designers and evaluators. We drew five lessons, as follows:

1. The kinds of changes desired by peace educators cannot be sustained in the face of adverse political events, belligerent environments, and the eroding forces of time in the absence of continued scaffolding and reinforcement of the changes.

2. A direct approach to help program participants step into their adversary's shoes and legitimize its perspective may arouse strong resistance during conflict as it may threaten participants' sense of righteousness. On the other hand, learning about another remote conflict may circumvent that obstacle. It paves the way for what Perkins and Salomon (1992) have called *high-road transfer*, which affords the opportunity for mindful abstraction—the creation of a bird's eye view of conflicts. Such a view enables the application of conclusions reached regarding the remote conflict to the proximal one. The indirect way appears to be an effective one.

3. Strong negative emotions interfere with the ability to examine and adopt the other side's perspective or show much empathy with it as such experiences (particularly during intractable conflict) often threaten one's sense of identity vis-à-vis that of the adversary. The gradual establishment of strong and empathic interpersonal relations may be a necessary precondition.

4. Adversaries come to joint peace education programs with incompatible, even opposing agendas and perceptions that need to be taken into consideration. It may well be the case that working through these differences, using group processes, can establish some common ground.

5. In turn, the establishment of common ground may lead to unanticipated and serendipitous worthwhile goals such as a deeper understanding of one's self and that of the other side.

These lessons may seem quite trivial in hindsight. Didn't we all know them without having to engage in costly research? Not really. Findings that lead to alternative lessons would have sounded equally reasonable and trivial in hindsight: Once minds have changed nothing will reverse the transformation, there is nothing as effective as a direct assault on one's stubborn beliefs, negative feelings pave the way for change, and so on. Much can be learned from good theorizing and thorough research that is applicable to the design and implementation of peace education programs, even if the research was carried out in the context of an intractable context. Lessons learned from research in such a context, while dealing with unique challenges, are likely to be applicable to peace education in other contexts.

References

Angelica, M. P. (1999). *Conflict resolution training in Cyprus*. Retrieved November 1, 2004, from http://www.cyprus-conflict.net/angelica%20rpt%20-%201.htm

Azar, E. E. (1990). The learning case. In E. E. Azar & J. W. Burton (Eds.), *The management of protracted social conflict: Theory and practice* (pp. 126–140). Brighton, UK: Wheatsheaf.

Bar-Natan, I. (2005). *Does friendship between adversaries generalize?* Unpublished Doctoral Dissertation, Haifa University.

Bar-On, D. (2000). *Bridging the gap*. Hamburg, Germany: Krober-Stiftung.

Bar-On, D., & Kassem, F. (2004). Storytelling as a way to work through intractable conflicts: The German-Jews experience and its relevance to the Palestinian–Israeli context. *Journal of Social Issues, 60*, 289–306.

Bar-Tal, D. (2000). *Shared beliefs in a society*. Thousand Oaks, CA: Sage.

Bar-Tal, D. (2002). The elusive nature of peace education. In G. Salomon & B. Nevo (Eds.), *Peace education: The concept, principles, and practices around the world* (pp. 27–36). Mahwah, NJ: Lawrence Erlbaum Associates, Inc.

Bar-Tal, D. (2004). Nature, rationale and effectiveness of education for coexistence. *Journal of Social Issues, 60*, 253–272.

Bar-Tal, D., & Salomon, G. (in press). Israeli-Jewish narratives of the Israeli–Palestinian Conflict: Evolvement, contents, functions and consequences. In R. Rotberg (Ed.), *History's Double Helix: The Intertwined Narratives of Israel/Palestine*.

Biton, Y. (2002). *Israeli and Palestinian's Understanding of "Peace" as a function of their participation in Peace Education programs*. Unpublished Doctoral Dissertation, Haifa University.

Bodine, R., & Crawford, D. (1998). *The handbook of conflict resolution education: A guide to building quality programs in schools*. San Francisco: Jossey-Bass.

Bruner, J. (1990). *Acts of meaning*. Cambridge, MA: Harvard University Press.

Cairns, E., & Hewstone, M. (2002). Northern Ireland: The impact of peacemaking in Northern Ireland on intergroup behavior. In G. Salomon & B. Nevo (Eds.), *Peace education: The concept, principles and practices around the world*. Mahwah, NJ: Lawrence Erlbaum Associates, Inc.

Coleman, P. T. (2003). Characteristics of protracted, intractable conflict: Toward the development of a metaframework-I. *Peace and Conflict, 9,* 1–38.

Deutsch, M. (1993). Educating for a peaceful world. *American Psychologist, 48,* 510–517.

Devine-Wright, P. (2001). History and identity in Northern Ireland: An exploratory investigation of the role of historical commemorations in context of intergroup conflict. *Peace and Conflict, 7,* 297–316.

Eagly, A., & Chaiken, S. (1993). *The psychology of attitudes*. Fort Worth, TX: Harcourt Brace Jovanovich.

Foster, K. (1999). *Fighting fictions: War, narrative and national identity*. London: Pluto.

Galtung, J. (1969). Violence, peace and peace research. *Journal of Peace Research, 6,* 167–191.

Hewstone, M., & Brown, R. (1986). Contact is not enough: An intergroup perspective on the contact hypothesis. In M. Hewstone & R. Brown (Eds.), *Contact and conflict in intergroup encounters* (pp. 1–44). New York: Basit and Blackwell.

Kilpatrick, R., & Leitch, R. (2004). Teachers' and pupils' educational experiences and school-based responses to the conflict in Northern Ireland. *Journal of Social Issues, 60,* 563–586.

Kruglanski, A. W. (2004). *The psychology of closed mindedness*. New York: Psychology.

Leippe, M., & Eisenstadt, D. (1994). Generalization of dissonance reduction: Decreasing prejudice through induced compliance. *Journal of Personality and Social Psychology, 67,* 395–413.

Liebkind, K., & McAlister, A. L. (1999). Extended contact through peer modeling to promote tolerance in Finland. *European Journal of Social Psychology, 29,* 765–780.

Lustig, I. (2002). *The effects of studying distal conflicts on the perception of a proximal one*. Unpublished masters thesis, University of Haifa (Hebrew).

Maoz, I. (2000). Multiple conflicts and competing agendas: A framework for conceptualizing structural encounters between groups in conflict—The case of a coexistence project of Jews and Palestinians in Israel. Peace and Conflict: *Journal of Peace Psychology, 6,* 135–156.

Maoz, I., & Bar-On, D. (2002). From working through the holocaust to current ethnic conflicts: Evaluating the TRT group workshop in Hamburg. *Group, 26,* 29–48.

Mikulincer, M., & Nizan, B. (1988). Causal attribution, cognitive interference, and the generalization of learned helplessness. *Journal of Personality and Social Psychology, 55,* 470–478.

Perkins, D. N., & Salomon, G. (1992). The science and art of transfer. In A. L. Costa, J. Bellanca, & R. Forgarty (Eds.), *If minds matter: A foreword to the future*. Volume 1 (pp. 201–210). Palatine, IL: Skylight.

Pettigrew, T. F. (1997). Generalized intergroup contact effects on prejudice. *Personality and Social Psychology Bulletin, 23,* 173–185.

Pettigrew, T. F. (1998). Intergroup contact theory. In J. T. Spence, J. M. Darley, & D. J. Foss (Eds.), *Annual Review of Psychology, 49,* 65–85.

Rapoport, A. (1974). *Conflict in man-made environments*. Harmonsdworth, UK: Penguin.

Roe, M. D., & Cairns, E. (2003). Memories in conflict: Review and a look to the future. In E. Cairns & M. D. Roe (Eds.), *The role of memory in ethnic conflict* (pp. 171–180). New York: Palgrave McMillan.

Roth, A. (2005). *Structuring the adversary's narrative during an intractable conflict as part of peace education through Internet-based exchanges*. Unpublished Master's thesis, Haifa University, Faculty of Education.

Rouhana, N. (1997). *Identities in conflict: Palestinian citizens in an ethnic Jewish state*. New Haven, CT: Yale University Press.

Rouhana, N., & Bar-Tal, D. (1998). Psychological dynamics of intractable ethnonational conflicts. The Israeli–Palestinian case. *American Psychologist, 53,* 761–770.

Salomon, G. (2002). The nature of peace education: Not all programs are created equal. In G. Salomon & B. Nevo (Eds.), *Peace Education: The concept, principles, and practices around the world* (pp. 2–14). Mahwah, NJ: Lawrence Erlbaum Associates, Inc.

Salomon, G. (2004). A narrative-based view of peace education. *Journal of Social Issues, 60*, 273–288.

Sandy, V. S., Bailey, S., & Sloane-Akwara, V. (2000). Impact on students: Conflict resolution education's proven benefits for students. In T. S. Jones & D. Kmita (Eds.), *Does it work? The case for conflict resolution education in our nation's schools*. Washington, DC: CREnet.

Sarason, I. G. (1975). Anxiety and self preoccupation. In I. G. Sarason & C. D. Spielberger (Eds.), *Stress and anxiety* (Vol. 2, pp. 27–44). Washington, DC: Hemisphere.

Sherif, M. (1966). *Group conflict and cooperation*. London: Routledge & Kagan Paul.

Staub, E. (2002). From healing past wounds to the development of inclusive caring: Contents and processes of peace education. In G. Salomon & B. Nevo (Eds.), *Peace Education, The concept, principles, and practices around the world* (pp. 73–88). Mahwah, NJ: Lawrence Erlbaum Associates, Inc.

Suleiman, R. (2004). Planned encounters between Palestinian and Israelis: A social–psychological perspective. *Journal of Social Issues, 60*, 323–338.

Tamari, S. (2002). How narratives of the *Naqba* have evolved in the memories of exiled Palestinians. *Palestine–Israel: Journal of Politics, Economics and Culture, 9*, 101–109.

Troebst, S. (1998). *Conflict in Kosovo: Failure of prevention? An analytical documentation, 1989–1998*. Flensburg, Germany: European Centre for Minority Issues Working Papers #1.

Weick, K. (2001). *Making sense of the organization*. Malten, MA: Blackwell.

Susan Opotow
Janet Gerson
Sarah Woodside

From Moral Exclusion to Moral Inclusion: Theory for Teaching Peace

This article presents Moral Exclusion Theory as a way to systematize the study of complex issues in peace education and to challenge the thinking that supports oppressive social structures. The authors define its 2 key concepts: moral exclusion, the limited applicability of justice underlying destructive conflicts and difficult social problems; and moral inclusion, the emphasis on fairness, resource sharing, and concern for the well-being of all underlying peace building. They demonstrate the relevance of Moral Exclusion Theory in 4 key areas of peace education: (a) education for coexistence, (b) education for human rights, (c) education for gender equality, and (d) education for environmentalism. They then describe 2 common issues faced by schools, bullying and textbook bias, to demonstrate that moral exclusion is common and how students and staff can redress it. The article concludes with the challenge to use peace education as a tool for moral inclusion and for bringing about a world in which justice applies to all.

Susan Opotow is a Professor in the Graduate Program in Dispute Resolution at the University of Massachusetts Boston. Janet Gerson is the Acting Director of Training for the Peace Education Center at Teachers College, Columbia University. Sarah Woodside is an MA Candidate in the Graduate Program in Dispute Resolution at the University of Massachussetts Boston.

Correspondence should be addressed to Susan Opotow, Graduate Program in Dispute Resolution, University of Massachusetts Boston. 100 Morrissey Blvd., Boston, MA 02125. E-mail: susan.opotow@umb.edu

THE WORLD CAN BE A frightening place. Each generation has seen too much violence and too many deaths. Many kinds of conflicts—international, regional, intergroup, and interpersonal—damage people, communities, and the natural world. Conflicts can also change the world, socially and ecologically, and prompt vast human migrations in response to political violence, poverty, and ethnic and religious tensions. Though dreams of peace are as old as humanity, a sustained peace remains elusive.

Consistent with the purpose of this journal, we—a psychology of injustice researcher, a peace educator, and a high school teacher who is a graduate student in conflict studies—bring a theoretical lens to peace education. We do so enthusiastically because theory offers teachers a systematic way to present complex issues. Theory proposes interconnections among related elements and suggests a sequence of steps that can achieve change. This article describes *moral exclusion theory* (Opotow, 1990, 1995) as a useful tool for peace education. As we will explain, *moral exclusion* captures the dynamics underlying destructive conflicts and difficult social problems, whereas its counterpart, *moral inclusion,* captures the dynamics of peace building in its emphasis on fairness, resource sharing, and concern for the well-being of all.

We begin this article by defining conflict and peace and describing their relevance to peace education. We then describe moral exclusion, moral inclusion, and their relevance to four interrelated areas of peace education: coexistence, human rights, gender equality, and environmentalism. Throughout, we identify Web-based resources for an integrated, dynamic peace education curriculum. The final section describes two common examples of moral exclusion in schools, bullying and textbook bias, and the potential of peace education to introduce a morally inclusive perspective in a school's way of doing things.

Educating for Peace

Just as *conflict* and *peace* are complex constructs, *peace education,* too, is complex and can be approached in many ways, depending on particular understandings of conflict and peace. It is prudent, then, to begin this article with brief definitions of these key constructs.

Conflict

Conflict is a ubiquitous and normal part of social living. Conflicts can be small or large, obvious or hidden, and brief or long lasting. They occur internationally, nationally, and locally. In schools, for example, conflicts occur in chronic or acute tensions among students, staff, and community members. They can involve such intractable issues as bullying, tracking, and educational equity (see Deutsch, 1993a, 1993b, for excellent papers on conflict in educational contexts).

Although conflicts are inevitable in social relations, people can approach conflict constructively as well as destructively (Deutsch, 1973). When approached constructively and cooperatively, conflicts can surface important issues and challenge injustice. Conflicts do not invariably lead to violence (Opotow, 2000). Even when cooperative processes fail, people can still voice their concerns through individual or collective opposition, protest, and nonviolent noncooperation (Sharp, 1973). Although violence is sometimes described as innate, 20 scientists, authors of the *Seville Statement on Nonviolence* (UNESCO, 1986), argued that organized violence does not have biological roots: "Biology does not condemn humanity to war. ... Just as 'wars begin in the minds of men,' peace also begins in our minds. The same species who invented war is capable of inventing peace." Rules and technologies of war clearly change over time and vary between traditions, illustrating that social learning and culture influence how conflict is understood and enacted.

Peace

Just as human nature is often portrayed as innately violent, peace is often portrayed as a tranquil, uncomplicated end state. This is a constricted and oversimplified view of peace. Peace is only partly the absence of war (*negative peace*) or a state of harmony and justice (*positive peace*). Fundamentally, peace is a long-term and gutsy project that seeks to bring about lasting and constructive change in institutions that maintain society (Haavelsrud, 1996). Said differently, peace is "a dynamic social process in which justice, equity, and respect for basic human rights are maximized, and violence, both physical and structural, is minimized" (Reardon & Cabezudo, 2002, p. 19). To endure, peace requires social conditions that foster individual and societal well-being. Achieving and maintaining these social conditions, in turn, requires grappling with the inevitable conflicts that challenge peace using processes that are nonviolent, collaborative, and life enhancing. Just as conflict surfaces differing perspectives and needs, peace building is an opportunity to rethink and reshape the prevailing status quo. This article argues that peace building as constructive social change is the process of moral inclusion.

Peace Education

As former UNESCO Director-General Federico Mayor (1999) described,

> The United Nations initiatives for a culture of peace mark a new stage: Instead of focusing exclusively on rebuilding societies after they have been torn apart by violence, the emphasis is placed on preventing violence by fostering a culture where conflicts are transformed into cooperation before they can degenerate into war and destruction. The key to the prevention of violence is education for nonviolence. This requires the mobilisation of education in its broadest sense—education throughout life and involving the mass media as much as traditional educational institutions. (p. 23)

Peace education should be designed to recognize, challenge, and change the thinking that has supported oppressive societal structures and, as we argue, moral exclusion. It should reveal conditions that trigger violence, ideological rivalries, and national policies that maintain arms races, military systems, and inequitable economic priorities (Reardon, 1988). The pedagogy of peace education should be "a philosophy and a process involving skills, including listening, reflection, problem-solving, cooperation and conflict resolution. The process involves empowering people with the skills, attitudes and knowledge to create a safe world and build a sustainable environment" (Harris & Morrison, 2003, p. 9).

Peace education is not limited to children. It is relevant to K–12 schools, undergraduate and graduate education, professional workshops and in-service training, adult classes, and in community and faith-based programs. As the Balkan Action Agenda for Sustainable Peace (*Global Partnership for the Prevention of Armed Conflict News*, 2004) stated,

> Peace education should be introduced into all sectors of society to strengthen the capacities of citizens and societies to deal with conflict non-violently, and to transform destructive conflict into dialogue. NGOs [non-governmental organizations] can be a strong partner to authorities and other stakeholders in developing peace education. (p. 4)

When *moral exclusion* and *moral inclusion* are core components of peace education curricula, they offer students a framework for understanding how a limited applicability of justice can fuel destructive conflict.

Moral Exclusion and Inclusion

Our *scope of justice* is the psychological boundary within which concerns about fairness govern our conduct (Deutsch, 1985; Opotow, 1990; Staub, 1990). A constricted scope of justice limits contexts in which fairness is applicable, whereas an expanded scope of justice extends justice further. Those who are inside this boundary for fairness are *morally included* and seen as deserving fair treatment. Those outside are *morally excluded*, beyond our moral concerns, and eligible for deprivation, exploitation, and other harms that might be ignored or condoned as normal, inevitable, and deserved. In escalated, destructive conflict, moral exclusion routinely justifies human rights violations and genocide (Opotow, 2001, 2002). Bystanders to injustice may also exclude victims from the scope of justice when they ignore or understate harms inflicted on others and do not intervene (Lerner, 1980; Opotow & Weiss, 2000).

As Table 1 indicates, moral exclusion can be subtle or blatant and it can be narrow or wide in extent. Each form of moral exclusion is distinct, but they have much in common. All are characterized by (a) seeing those excluded as psychologically distant from and unconnected with oneself; (b) lacking constructive moral obligations toward those excluded; (c) viewing those excluded as nonentities, expendable, and undeserving of fair-

Table 1
Forms of Moral Exclusion

Extent of Moral Exclusion	Manifestations of Moral Exclusion	
	Subtle	Blatant
Narrow	Rudeness, intimidation, and derogation (e.g., bullying and sexual harassment)	Persecution and violence directed at particular individuals or groups (e.g., hate crimes, witch hunts)
Wide	Oppression and structural violence (e.g., racism, sweatshops, poverty, domestic violence)	Direct violence and violations of human rights (e.g., ethnic cleansing, mass murder, inquisitions)

Note. Adapted from Opotow, 2001.

ness and community resources that could foster their well-being; and (d) approving of procedures and outcomes for those excluded that would be unacceptable for those inside the scope of justice.

In extreme harmdoing, moral exclusion is blatant. But moral exclusion can be subtle and difficult to detect when it is socially condoned. Even when it is subtle, moral exclusion is evident in a number of symptoms, described in Table 2, which include dehumanization, fearing contamination from social contact, reducing one's moral standards, normalizing violence, displacement of responsibility, and psychological distancing.

From Moral Exclusion to Moral Inclusion

Achieving a stable peace based on social justice requires a shift from moral exclusion to moral inclusion. Peace is possible "when society agrees that the overarching purpose of public policies is the achievement and maintenance of mutually beneficial circumstances that enhance the life possibilities of all" (Reardon, 2001, p. 5).

Moral inclusion is a fundamental and strategic principle of peace education because it means the willingness to (a) extend fairness to others, (b) allocate resources to them, and (c) make sacrifices that would foster their well-being (Opotow, 1990). For moral inclusion to be effective, it needs to be substantial and sustained so that all levels of society, from grassroots to state-level, and all subpopulations, including people who are illiterate and from remote areas, are included in the process of social change and share in social resources (Opotow, 2002). If moral inclusion is superficial, narrow, or short lived, it can disappoint, recreate unjust conditions, and result in destructive conflict and war.

Applying Moral Exclusion/Inclusion in Peace Education

Educators can use Moral Exclusion Theory to systematize their study of conflict, war, and peace. We illustrate this in four interrelated social problems that are key areas of peace education: education for coexistence, education for human rights, education for gender equality, and education for environmentalism. We also provide links that suggest the array of Internet resources that educators can use in their curriculum (see Appendix A).

Educating for Coexistence

Educating for coexistence (also called *diversity education* and *multicultural education*) addresses acute and chronic between-group tensions fostered by religious and ethnic intolerance. Consistent with research on ethnocentric conflict (Stephan & Stephan, 1996), groups in conflict have derogatory stereotypes about each other that justify excluding members of opposing groups from their scope of justice. Due to self-serving biases, violent behavior of one's own group is seen

Table 2
Symptoms of Moral Exclusion

Symptom	Description
Double standards	Having different norms for different groups
Concealing effects of harmful outcomes	Disregarding, ignoring, distorting, or minimizing injurious outcomes that others experience
Reducing moral standards	Asserting that one's harmful behavior is proper while denying one's lesser concern for others
Utilizing euphemisms	Masking and sanitizing harmful behavior and outcomes
Biased evaluation of groups	Making unflattering between-group comparisons that bolster one's own group at the expense of others
Condescension and derogation	Regarding others with disdain
Dehumanization	Denying others' rights, entitlements, humanity, and dignity
Fear of contamination	Perceiving contact or alliances with other stakeholders as posing a threat to oneself
Normalization and glorification of violence	Glorifying and normalizing violence; viewing violence as an effective, legitimate, or even sublime form of human behavior while denying the potential of violence to damage people, the environment, relationships, and constructive conflict resolution processes
Victim blaming	Placing blame on those who are harmed
Deindividuation	Believing one's contribution to social problems is undetectable
Diffusing responsibility	Denying personal responsibility for harms by seeing them as the result of collective rather than individual decisions and actions
Displacing responsibility	Identifying others, such as subordinates or supervisors, as responsible for harms inflicted on victims

Note. Adapted from Opotow, 1990 and Opotow & Weiss, 2000.

as appropriate and fair whereas analogous behavior by an opponent is seen as abhorrent and provocative (Opotow, 2001; White, 1984).

Educating for coexistence seeks to replace dehumanizing stereotypes, chronic distrust, hostility, violence, and moral exclusion with, first, tolerance and minimal cooperation and, ultimately, with moral inclusion—increasing the applicability of justice, sharing of resources, and making sacrifices that could foster joint well-being. Dialogue groups, sharing personal narratives, and collaborating on mutually beneficial projects are methods that promote coexistence by increasing trust and cooperation through positive contacts among members of conflicting groups (Maoz, 2005).

Coexistence education can be a learning experience. However, because one party in conflict often has more power than the other, coexistence education may have different meaning for groups with more and less power (Gerson & Opotow, 2004). Due to conventional economic and political arrangements, members of low-power groups within social structures often serve and observe members of high-power groups and therefore have an expert understanding that helps them to survive (Kidder, 2000). Coexistence education can be an opportunity for this awareness to become mutual. If members of high-power groups can learn to humanize rather than ignore or disparage members of low-power groups and then come to see the inequitable distribution of privilege and disadvantage within their society, it can stimulate an understanding of how moral exclusion is normalized by existing power arrangements and the long-term negative effects of these arrangements on individuals, families, communities, and nations. In spite of positive changes that can result from coexistence education, however, between-group tensions may remain when coexistence efforts that occur at the micro-level do not translate into macro-level structural change (Bar-On, 2000).

Educating for Human Rights

Blatant examples of human rights violations include "extrajudicial killing, genocide, disappearance, rape, torture, and severe ill treatment" (Crocker, 2000, p. 99). These violations of civil and political rights are one of three categories of human rights (http://www.abc.net.au/civics/rights/what.htm):

1. *Civil and political rights*, including the right to life, liberty, and security; political participation; freedom of opinion, expression, thought, conscience, and religion; freedom of association and assembly; and freedom from torture and slavery.
2. *Economic and social rights*, including the right to work; education; a reasonable standard of living; food; shelter and health care.
3. *Environmental, cultural, and developmental rights*, including the right to live in an environment that is clean and protected from destruction, and rights to cultural, political, and economic development.

Human rights are universal and inviolable. This means that they apply to everyone regardless of gender, age, ethnicity, religion, nationality, and political or other beliefs, and they cannot be taken away, as described in the *Universal Declaration of Human Rights* (http://www.un.org/Overview/rights.html).[1] Peace education for human rights not only studies violations, but it also studies standards delineated in such documents as the *Universal Declaration of Human Rights*, international treaties negotiated through the United Nations system,[2] and statutes of international courts. Human rights, as detailed in these documents, may seem abstract, but they come alive when students study the genocide in Rwanda, civilian deaths in Iraq, and torture of prisoners in Abu-Ghraib and prisons throughout the world. Students, their families, and members of their communities may themselves have experienced human rights violations resulting from racism, apartheid, or political, ethnic, religious, or gender violence.

In addition to learning from vivid, powerful historical and contemporary examples of human rights violations and from personal experiences, educating for human rights promotes moral inclusion when students learn to recognize less obvious aspects of human rights—the politics that devise, support, and conceal human rights abuses (Opotow, 2002). Students learn to recognize contradictions between a rhetoric supporting human rights and the failure to protect victims or punish violators. These gaps identify opportunities for bystanders—individuals, groups, communities, and nations—to act for social justice.

Educating for Gender Equality

Peace education for gender equality focuses on injustice and violence experienced by women and girls in interpersonal, community, institutional, and societal contexts. Gender-related injustice can be a pervasive yet invisible problem in oppressive, violent, and exploitative relationships at home, at work, and in the larger community. Internationally, it includes female infanticide (Sen, 1999), trafficking of women and girls in the sex trade (Shahinian, 2002), and the intentional use of violence and rape in war (McKay, 1998). Gender inequality and violence excludes or diminishes the participation of half of humanity from economic, political, legal, and social affairs.

Throughout the world, women are poorer and are less likely to be educated than men. In many countries, women may not inherit family wealth or own land, perpetuating their disadvantage and dependence. Women experience discrimination in societies characterized by violations of the basic human rights to self-determination and misogyny, but they also experience discrimination in more egalitarian societies when women work longer hours than men, earn lower wages, and carry a larger share of housework (http://www.esrc.ac.uk/ESRCContent/news/feb05–5.asp). Even among children, boys have more leisure time whereas girls do more household chores (Unger & Crawford, 1992).

Disadvantaged in peace (Denmark, Rabinowitz, & Sechzer, 2000), women are even more disadvantaged in war. They are overrepresented among victims of conflict, and, in postconflict reconstruction efforts, they are underrepresented as decision-makers, administrators, and judges (McKay, 1998; Morris, 1998). Rape as a tactic of war (e.g., in Bosnia, Rwanda, Sierra Leone, and Indonesia) has long-lasting negative sequelae for victims who survive and are then ostracized by families or communities (Swiss & Giller, 1993). Poverty, an inadequate diet, a heavy workload made heavier by family deaths, unresolved grief, continuous harassment, and fear of further violence also compromise women's physical and mental health as a result of war (Zur, 1996).

Peace education for gender equality focuses on disparities (e.g., income, health, and decision-making responsibility) between men and women and examines the assumptions, traditions, and oppressive structural arrangements that systematically disadvantage women. Students learn to critically examine a variety of social contexts and to question who speaks, who decides, who benefits, who is absent, and who is expected to make sacrifices. These critical analyses can reveal gender inequalities and moral exclusion that permeate daily life locally, nationally, and globally, and suggest ways to increase moral inclusion. As the result of persistent and collaborative activism, moral inclusion of women has increased and, to some extent, been institutionalized throughout the world in governmental policies, national and international laws,[3] and in more accurate reporting of violations. These structural changes build on one another and offer students hope for furthering gender balance and social justice.

Educating for Environmentalism

Environmental issues present an urgent challenge throughout the world. Air, water, and land pollution, and the overuse of natural resources continue at alarming rates, increasingly straining the Earth's capacity to sustain healthy ecosystems and human life. Damage to the natural world results from the way we go about our daily lives, commercial uses of natural resources and byproducts of industry, as well as war and military activities (e.g., nuclear testing). Environmental degradation is often viewed as a technological problem with technological solutions (e.g., the development of renewable energy resources), but it is also a psychological problem because it results from the way we understand our relationship to nature (Clayton & Opotow, 2003). Environmental protection is less likely when we see ourselves as unconnected to and outside of nature. When nature is excluded from our scope of justice we can deny the severity, extent, and irreversibility of environmental destruction, deny the entitlements of other people, future generations, and nonhuman entities to natural resources, and deny our own role—as individuals and collectives—in advancing environmental degradation.

Environmentalism refers to environmentally protective attitudes, positions, and behavior. Educating for environmentalism focuses on the exploitation and degradation of the natural world as critical problems. It extends peace education beyond human groups to the inclusion of the Earth, its animals, plants, inanimate habitats, and commons (e.g., air, rivers, oceans) within the scope of justice (Leopold, 1949). Environmentalism promotes moral inclusion when it prompts a rethinking of our relationship with and responsibility toward diverse aspects of nature. Environmental conservation is more complex than simply protecting nature. To be effective it requires recognizing the needs, interests, and perspectives of a variety of people. Considering other environmental stakeholders (human and nonhuman) within the realm of what matters to us can offer broad-based and long-term support for environmental conservation (Opotow & Brook, 2003). International treaties[4] stress ecological awareness and cooperation to deter environmental degradation and promote conservation. The Living Systems Model, developed by ecologists and used in peace education, emphasizes the interdependence and vulnerability of living systems and the importance of caring for all living beings and systems, including those that cannot act on their own behalf. This model challenges the idea of security as military force and argues for security that depends on interdependence and caring for those who are vulnerable (Gerson et al., 1997). Children throughout the world, from urban and rural communities and from well-to-do and poor families, have participated in educational projects in schools. These projects promote environmentalism through studying and advocating for recycling, composting, and wise disposal of waste. Students have also mapped their community's ecological and cultural resources as a learning and activist project that emphasizes the connection between local environmental issues and the development of sustainable communities (Hart, 1997).

In summary, when moral exclusion and moral inclusion are core components of educating for coexistence, human rights, gender equality, and environmentalism, they direct students' attention to assumptions, stereotypes, and societal arrangements that fuel destructive conflict and war. A peace education pedagogy that exposes moral exclusion and promotes moral inclusion will encourage critical inquiry and experiential learning as the forerunner of constructive societal change.

Walking the Talk: Bringing Peace Education Home

Well-designed peace education programs (see examples in Apendix A) convey useful information and pedagogical approaches. Generic programs, however, cannot address issues faced by particular students or schools, such as hostility directed at Muslim students after 9/11 (http://school.discovery.com/lessonplans/pdf/911backlash/911backlash.pdf), students who are "out" about their sexual orientation and face peer rejection (Griffin & Ouellett, 2003), or students who feel excluded when they are labeled as academically inadequate (Sanon, Baxter, Fortune, & Opotow, 2001). Two issues, bullying and textbook bias, illustrate how peace education, informed by moral exclusion theory, can replace an exclusionary status quo with more inclusionary attitudes and actions.

Bullying

In bullying, harassment, and violence systematically intimidate and disrupt the well-being of victims. Bullying is common; 1 in 10 students are harassed regularly (Olweus, 1993). Bullying has negative consequences for victims, bystanders, and institutions (e.g., work, jails, schools) in which it occurs.

Bullying can negatively affect a school's climate by normalizing interpersonal aggression. It can be pervasive yet remain unaddressed by school staff or the peace education curriculum. A program developed and tested in Norway illustrates how bullying can be halted to change a school climate from fear and violence to respect and safety (Olweus, 1993). This program operationalizes moral inclusion by emphasizing a school, home, and community culture characterized by warmth toward and positive interest in children; support and protection for victims; clear limits on unacceptable, antisocial behavior; clear and consistently applied nonhostile sanctions for rule violations; and appropriate observation of student activities. It has been replicated to prevent or reduce bullying in elementary, middle, and junior high schools (http://modelprograms.samhsa.gov/pdfs/ FactSheets/Olweus%20Bully.pdf; http://www. sjs.sd83.bc.ca/safe/bully.htm).

Textbooks

Educational materials have the potential to foster stereotyping and exclusion; they can also foster mutual understanding. A textbook project in Afghanistan seeks to replace religious and warlike themes with themes promoting peace, stability, and human rights (Gall, 2004). A collaborative project of Teachers College of Columbia University, the United Nations Children's Fund, and the Afghanistan Ministry of Education, will publish texts in four local languages and introduce a teaching style new to Afghanistan that encourages student participation and active, experiential learning rather than rote memorization.

In PRIME's[5] *Writing the Shared History* project in Israel, Jewish and Palestinian teachers and historians worked collaboratively to design a textbook to "disarm the teaching of Middle East history in Israeli and Palestinian classrooms" (http://vispo.com/PRIME/leohn.htm). It has published a graphically striking history book, focused on several periods of national conflict. Each page is divided into thirds. One column describes the Palestinian perspective in Arabic; another column describes the Jewish perspective in Hebrew. A third column is blank, encouraging students to write about the same period as it affected their own family or community (http://www.beyondintractability.org/iweb/audio/chaitin-j.html). This approach emphasizes how history affects differently situated people as well as the importance of one's own standpoint for interpreting historical events (Collins, 2004). Recognizing that textbooks can influence and change attitudes, both projects operationalize moral inclusion by challenging stereotypes and widening the scope of justice.

Peace educators can also encourage students to critically examine their own educational materials for exclusionary attitudes. Howard Zinn's *A People's History of the United States* (1980), for example, presents history from the perspective of oppressed people. This approach is instructive because it presents an underrepresented perspective. For students from resource-poor groups, critical examination of history can bring their own community's experiences into the classroom in ways that make learning come alive (Pratt, 1991; http://web.nwe.ufl.edu/~stripp/2504/pratt.html). For students from resource-rich groups, critical examination can challenge widely accepted and self-serving myths of superiority, accomplishment, and valor, educating students about perspectives they may have never considered (Fine & Weis, 2001).

Conclusion

Georg Simmel (1955) has observed that "the transition from war to peace constitutes a more serious problem than does the reverse" (p. 109). Peace education seeks to effect this difficult shift from spiraling deadly conflict to an inclusionary orientation for individuals, groups, and larger collectives. Rather than see moral exclusion as something done by bad people, it is important to understand it as a human capacity—something we all do (Opotow, 1995). Peace education programs can sharpen critical skills, examine taken-for-granted assumptions, and rethink the status quo. Peace education itself sometimes suffers from moral exclusion in schools when it is dismissed as wishy-washy and touchy-feely by teachers or administrators. Coupling moral exclusion theory with such crucial issues as coexistence, human rights, gender equality, and environmentalism makes it clear that peace education addresses grave, timely, and relevant topics that need to be studied by students of all ages.

Consistent with PRIME's *Writing the Shared History* project and the Afghan text project, students need to actively participate in their education. Most students experience the complexity of social relations in conflicts with peers. Because these conflicts engage participants (and often, bystanders) they also have pedagogical potential (Opotow, 1991). At the core of these conflicts are moral questions concerning right and wrong, responsibilities, and acceptable social norms. Because these conflicts generate discomfort and can take an unpredictable course, they can motivate learning about communication, perspective taking, and problem solving. They also offer junctures for students to engage with adults to learn about themselves, crucial conflict resolution skills, and the relationship between everyday conflict and peace (Opotow, 2004).

This article urges attention to all levels of conflict, from the interpersonal and local to the international. To be effective, peace education should avoid a constricted focus that romanticizes an unsustainable, tranquil vision of peace. Instead it should capture the dynamic and pressing nature of social tensions and mobilize this urgency to reexamine social arrangements that institutionalize inequality and injustice. Peace education as moral inclusion challenges us to imagine how things could be different as a result of widening the applicability of justice to people throughout the world and to the nonhuman natural world. It also entails action. Utilizing natural, social, and manmade resources more cautiously and the willingness to share resources to reduce inequality is at the heart of an inclusive and dynamic peace education.

Notes

1. Also see http://www.sjs.sd83.bc.ca/h-rights/h-rights.htm for a one-page summary of human rights on a Canadian middle school Web site.
2. *The Universal Declaration of Human Rights* (UDHR) was adopted by the General Assembly of the United Nations in 1948. Specialized human rights treaties include *Convention on the Elimination of All Forms of Racial Discrimination* (1966); the *Convention Against Torture and Other Cruel, Inhuman and Degrading Treatment or Punishment* (1984); and the *Convention on the Rights of the Child* (1989).
3. *The Convention on the Elimination of All Forms of Discrimination against Women* (CEDAW) was adopted by the UN General Assembly in 1979 and entered into force in 1981. Described as an international bill of rights for women, it defines discrimination against women and sets up an agenda for national action to end such discrimination (see http://www.un.org/womenwatch/daw/ and http://www.unifem.org/ for updates on challenges to gender equality and progress in redressing these challenges).
4. For example, the *Rio Summit on Sustainable Development* (1992), the *Earth Summit+5* (1997) and the *Johannesburg Summit Rio+10* (2002).
5. Peace Research Institute in the Middle East

References

Bar-On, D. (Ed.). (2000). *Bridging the gap: Storytelling as a way to work through political and collective hostilities.* Hamburg, Germany: Körber-Stiftung.

Clayton, S., & Opotow, S. (2003). Introduction: Identity and the natural environment. In S. Clayton & S. Opotow (Eds.), *Identity and the natural environment: The psychological significance of nature* (pp. 1–24). Cambridge, MA: MIT Press.

Collins, P. H. (2004). Learning from the outsider within: The sociological significance of Black feminist thought. In S. Harding (Ed.), *The feminist standpoint theory reader* (pp. 103–126). New York: Routledge.

Crocker, D. A. (2000). Truth commissions, transitional justice, and civil society. In R. I. Rotberg & D. Thompson (Eds.), *Truth v. justice: The morality of truth commissions.* Princeton, NJ: Princeton University Press.

Denmark, F., Rabinowitz, V., & Sechzer, J. (2000). *Engendering psychology.* Needham Heights, MA: Allyn & Bacon.

Deutsch, M. (1973). *The resolution of conflict.* New Haven, CT: Yale University Press.

Deutsch, M. (1985). *Distributive justice: A social psychological perspective.* New Haven, CT: Yale University Press.

Deutsch, M. (1993a). Educating for a peaceful world. *American Psychologist, 48,* 510–517.

Deutsch, M. (1993b). Conflict resolution and cooperative learning in an alternative high school. *Cooperative Learning, 14*(4), 2–5.

Fine, M., & Weis, L. (2001). *Construction sites: Excavating race, class and gender with urban youth.* New York: Teachers College Press.

Gall, C. (2004, December 27). Afghan students are back, but not the old textbooks. *The New York Times,* A11.

Gerson, J., Gubuan, D., Magno, C., Nakano, M., Newton, S., & Susa, F. (1997, Winter). Codes for interpersonal and group relations in a world of conflict and change. *Holistic Education Review, 10*(4), 26–34.

Gerson, J., & Opotow, S. (2004). Deadly conflict and the challenge of coexistence. Book review of G. Salomon & B. Nevo (Eds.). (2002). *Peace education: The concept, principles, and practices around the world.* Mahwah, NJ: Lawrence Erlbaum Associates, Inc. In *Analyses of Social Issues and Public Policy, 4,* 265–268.

Global Partnership for the Prevention of Armed Conflict News. (2004, Dec.). The Balkan Action Agenda for Sustainable Peace. Retrieved January 31, 2005, from http://www.gppac.org/documents/GPPAC/News/news4.pdf

Griffin, P., & Ouellett, M. (2003). From silence to safety and beyond: Historical trends in addressing lesbian, gay, bisexual, transgender issues in K–12 schools. *Equity & Excellence in Education, 36,* 106–114.

Haavelsrud, M. (1996). *Education in developments.* Oslo, Norway: Arena.

Harris, I. M., & Morrison, M. L. (2003). *Peace education* (2nd ed.). Jefferson, NC: McFarland.

Hart, R. (1997). *Children's participation: The theory and practice of involving young citizens in community development and environmental care.* London: Earthscan and New York: UNICEF.

Kidder, L. H. (2000). Dependents in the master's house: When rock dulls scissors. In S. Dickey & K. M. Adams (Eds.), *Home and hegemony: Domestic service and identity politics in South and Southeast Asia* (pp. 207–220). Ann Arbor: University of Michigan.

Leopold, A. (1949). *A Sand County almanac, and sketches here and there.* New York: Oxford University.

Lerner, M. (1980). *Belief in a just world.* New York: Plenum.

Maoz, I. (2005). Evaluating the communication between groups in dispute: Equality in contact interventions between Jews and Arabs in Israel. *Negotiation Journal, 21,* 131–146.

Mayor, F. (1999). Toward a new culture of peace and non-violence. In *People building peace: 35 inspiring stories from around the world.* Utrecht, The Netherlands: European Centre for Conflict Prevention.

McKay, S. (1998). The effects of armed conflict on girls and women. *Peace and Conflict: Journal of Peace Psychology, 4,* 381–392.

Morris, P. T. (1998, July). *Weaving gender in disaster and refugee assistance.* Washington, DC: InterAction.

Olweus, D. (1993). *Bullying at school: What we know and what we can do.* Cambridge, MA: Blackwell.

Opotow, S. (1990). Moral exclusion and injustice: An overview. *Journal of Social Issues, 46*(1), 1–20.

Opotow, S. (1991). Adolescent peer conflicts: Implications for students and for schools. *Education and Urban Society, 23,* 416–441.

Opotow, S. (1995). Drawing the line: Social categorization, moral exclusion, and the scope of justice. In B. B. Bunker & J. Z. Rubin (Eds.), *Conflict, cooperation, and justice* (pp. 347–369). San Francisco: Jossey-Bass.

Opotow, S. (2000). Aggression and violence. In M. Deutsch & P. Coleman (Eds.), *The handbook of conflict resolution: Theory and practice* (pp. 403–427). San Francisco: Jossey Bass.

Opotow, S. (2001). Social injustice. In D. J. Christie, R. V. Wagner, & D. D. Winter (Eds.), *Peace, conflict and violence: Peace psychology for the 21st century* (pp. 102–109). New York: Prentice-Hall.

Opotow, S. (2002). The psychology of impunity and injustice: Implications for social reconciliation. In M. C. Bassiouni (Ed.), *Post conflict justice* (pp. 201–216). Ardsley, NY: Transnational.

Opotow, S. (2004). Conflict and morals. In T. A. Thorkildsen, J. Manning, & H. J. Manning (Eds.), *Nurturing morality.* New York: Kluwer.

Opotow, S., & Brook, A. (2003). Identity and exclusion in rangeland conflict. In S. Clayton & S. Opotow (Eds.), *Identity and the natural environment: The psychological significance of nature* (pp. 249–272). Cambridge, MA: MIT Press.

Opotow, S., & Weiss, L. (2000). Denial and exclusion in environmental conflict. *Journal of Social Issues, 56,* 475–490.

Pratt, M. L. (1991). Arts of the contact zone. *Profession, 91,* 33–40.

Reardon, B. (2001). *Educating for a culture of peace in a gender perspective.* Paris: UNESCO.

Reardon, B. (1988). *Comprehensive peace education: Educating for global responsibility.* New York: Teachers College Press.

Reardon, B. A., & Cabezudo, A. (2002). *Rationale for and approaches to peace education. Book 1: Learning to abolish war —Teaching toward a culture of peace.* New York: Hague Appeal for Peace.

Sanon, F., Baxter, M., Fortune, L., & Opotow, S. (2001). Cutting class: Perspectives of urban high school students. In J. Shultz & A. Sather-Cook (Eds.), *In our own words: Students' perspectives on school* (pp. 73–91). Boulder, CO: Rowman & Littlefield.

Sen, A. (1999). *Development as freedom.* New York: Alfred A. Knopf.

Shahinian, G. (2002). *Trafficking in women and girls.* Retrieved February 1, 2004, from http://www.un.org/womenwatch/daw/egm/trafficking2002/reports/EP-Shahinian.PDF

Sharp, G. (1973). *The politics of nonviolent action: Part II—The methods of nonviolent action.* Boston: Porter Sargent (see also *The methods of nonviolent action*; retrieved November 30, 2004, from http://www.peacemagazine.org/198.htm).

Simmel, G. (1955). *Conflict.* New York: Free Press.

Staub, E. (1990). Moral exclusion, personal goal theory, and extreme destructiveness. *Journal of Social Issues, 46*(1), 47–64.

Stephan, W. G., & Stephan, C. W. (1996). *Intergroup relations.* Boulder, CO: Westview.

Swiss, S., & Giller, J. (1993). Rape as a crime of war: A medical perspective. *Journal of the American Medical Association, 270,* 612–615.

UNESCO. (1986). *The Seville statement on nonviolence.* Retrieved November 22, 2004, from http://portal.unesco.org/education/en/ev.php-URL_ID=3247&URL_DO=DO_TOPIC&URL_SECTION=201.html

Unger, R., & Crawford, M. (1992). *Women and gender.* Philadelphia: Temple University Press.

White, R. K. (1984). *Fearful warriors: A psychological profile of U.S.–Soviet Relations.* New York: The Free Press.

Zinn, H. (1980). *A people's history of the United States.* New York: Harper & Row.

Zur, J. (1996). From PTSD to voices in context: From an "experience-far" to an "experience-near" understanding of responses to war and atrocity across cultures. *International Journal of Social Psychiatry, 42,* 305–317.

Appendix A
Annotated Resource for Peace Educators

A. General Information: Peace Education

A1. Informative Web sites:

OXFAM network	http://www.oxnet.org	Forum for individuals to share resources
Psychologists for Social Responsibility, Peace Education Action Committee	http://www.psysr.org/peace%20education%20AC.htm	Information about peace education resources and application of psychological knowledge to peace education
World Council for Curriculum and Instruction	http://www.alliant.edu/gsoe/wcci	International issues from theoretical and practical perspectives

A2. Web sites presenting curricula:

Free the Children	http://www.freethechildren.org	Advocacy projects created by and for youth
Hague Appeal for Peace: Global Campaign for Peace Education	http://www.haguepeace.org/peaceeducation/hapresources.php	Curriculum, resources, and advocacy materials
Oxfam	http://www.oxfam.ca/education	Teachable resources on world issues

B. Educating for Coexistence (e.g., tolerance, coexistence, racism, gender equality, healthy relationships, social justice, multiculturalism)

B1. Informative Web sites:

Racism No Way	http://www.racismnoway.com.au	Classroom materials to help recognize and eliminate racism
Southern Poverty Law Center Web Project	http://www.tolerance.org	Resources for schools and teachers on teaching tolerance
United Nations Cyberschoolbus	http://www.un.org/pubs/cyberschoolbus	Teaching materials for educational use and training teachers; promotes education about international issues
United Nations Education, Social, and Cultural Organization	http://portal.unesco.org	Materials on tolerance, learning to live together, and other educational resources
Women's Educational Media	http://www.womedia.org/ourfilms.htm	Films for teaching inclusion of diverse groups

(continued)

Appendix A (Continued)

B2. Web sites presenting curricula:

Center for Holocaust and Genocide Studies	http://www.chgs.umn.edu/CoexistenceCurriculum.pdf	Lessons for using visual arts to teach coexistence
Educators for Social Responsibility, National	http://www.esrnational.org/home.htm	Lessons for teaching conflict resolution and inclusion with a national and international emphasis
Educators for Social Responsibility, New York City	http://www.esrmetro.org	Lessons for teaching conflict resolution and inclusion developed for urban schools
Men for Change	http://www.chebucto.ns.ca/CommunitySupport/Men4Change/m4ccuric.html	Lessons for promoting positive masculinity and ending sexism and violence
Social Justice Education	http://www.socialjusticeeducation.org	Lessons and advocacy opportunities for social justice and learning to organize for social change

C. Educating for Human Rights (e.g., rights of refugees, women, crimes against humanity and genocide, comprehensive human rights, equal opportunity, indigenous rights)

C1. Informative Web sites:

Center for Constitutional Rights	http://www.ccr-ny.org	U.S. and international legal issues presented in reports, publications and other resources
Derechos	http://www.derechos.org	Human rights network and resource site
Human Rights Internet	http://www.hri.ca/index.aspx	Internet links to human rights resources
International Network for Economic, Social and Cultural Rights	http://www.escr-net.org	International chat room for human rights activists to exchange information and ideas
People's Movement for Human Rights Education	http://www.pdhre.org	Resources on human rights education and advocacy
United Nations and the International Criminal Court (ICC)	http://www.un.org/law/icc	Statutes of the International Criminal Court that define crimes of humanity and war crimes
UNESCO Human Rights Education	http://portal.unesco.org/education/en/ev.php-URL_ID=1920&URL_DO=DO_TOPIC&URL_SECTION=201.html	Human rights documents including declarations, covenants, conventions, protocols, and platforms for action

C2. Web sites presenting curricula:

Australian Broadcasting Corporation, Department of Education and Training	http://www.abc.net.au/civics/rights	Teaching materials and case studies on refugee, women's, and indigenous rights
Australian Human Rights and Equal Opportunity Commission	http://www.hreoc.gov.au	Teacher and student resources on racism, sexism, indigenous, and disabilities rights
United Nations High Commission on Refugees	http://www.unhcr.ch/cgi-bin/texis/vtx/help?id=407f1382	Teaching materials on refugee issues including curricula, games, and information brochures
U. of Minnesota Human Rights Resource Center	http://www1.umn.edu/humanrts/edumat	Curricula, topic guides, fact sheets and featured lessons on human rights

D. Educating for Gender Equality (e.g., gender equality, training and development, sex discrimination, law, men's roles in gender equality, advocacy)

D1. Informative Web sites:

Canadian International Development Agency	http://www.acdi-cida.gc.ca/equality	Tools for integrating gender equality into education and the workplace
CEDAW: Treaty on the Status of Women	http://www.cedaw.org	UN Convention on the Elimination of All Forms of Discrimination Against Women and updates on its ratification
Commission on the Status of Women	http://www.un.org/womenwatch/daw/csw	Recommendations to the UN on promoting women's rights in the political and other arenas
Men's Bibliography	http://www.mensbiblio.xyonline.net/activism.html	Resources for social change
San Francisco Commission on the Status of Women	http://www.sfgov.org/site/dosw_page.asp?id=19794	The City of San Francisco's official document on eliminating discrimination against women. Models how a city can develop laws to foster gender inclusion.
UNIFEM-United Nations Development Fund for Women	http://www.unifem.org	Resources on the use of international treaties and law to build legal protection for women
Women's Human Rights Resources	http://www.law-lib.utoronto.ca/Diana	Resources, fact sheets, and advocacy guides on international women's rights law

(continued)

Appendix A (*Continued*)

D2. Web sites presenting curricula:

Amnesty International—USA	http://www.amnestyusa.org/education	Human rights teaching guides, lesson plans, and Urgent Actions geared to students
Human Rights Watch	http://www.hrw.org/women/trafficking.html	Reports and advocacy programs against trafficking of women and girls
White Ribbon Campaign	http://www.whiteribbon.ca/educational_materials	Lesson plans to explore attitudes/behavior that contribute to men's exclusion of women

E. Educating for Environmentalism

E1. Informative Web sites:

Earth Charter	http://www.earthcharter.org	Information on the Earth Charter, a teaching resource database and resources for youth groups
Earth Summit+5	http://www.un.org/esa/earthsummit/ and http://www.un.org/documents/ga/res/spec/aress19-2.htm	Information and program of action from the Earth Summit +5 The UN General Assembly Resolution for the Programme for Implementation of Agenda 21+5
Rio Earth Summit 1992	http://www.un.org/geninfo/bp/enviro.html	Information about the 1992 Rio Earth Summit

E2. Web sites presenting curricula:

Earth Charter	http://www.earthcharter.org/resources	Lessons and activities for teaching about the Earth Charter
Green Map System (GMS)	http://www.greenmap.org	Rationale and activities for making local maps of ecological and cultural resources and degradation
UNESCO	http://www.unesco.org/education/tlsf	Resources and curriculum for a sustainable environment
YouthCaN	http://www.youthcanworld.org	Youth run organization; activities and projects concerning environmental issues to inspire, educate and connect youth

Elizabeth A. Gassin
Robert D. Enright
Jeanette A. Knutson

Bringing Peace to the Central City: Forgiveness Education in Milwaukee

The last 2 decades have seen a flowering of scholarly and applied work in the area of forgiveness, a skill important to the development of peaceful people and communities. We describe a forgiveness intervention designed to help children in a central-city environment. Such environments put children at risk for various psychological and social problems, including antisocial behavior, in large part because of the many forms of injustice experienced in such a context. Injustice often leads to anger, a key emotion in the development of psychological, interpersonal, and even academic problems. The current forgiveness education program is showing promise in Belfast, Northern Ireland, and is now being implemented in inner-city Milwaukee.

Elizabeth A. Gassin is an Assistant Professor in the Department of Psychology at Olivet Nazarene University. Robert D. Enright is a Professor in the Department of Educational Psychology at the University of Wisconsin–Madison. Jeanette A. Knutson works at the International Forgiveness Institute.

Correspondence should be addressed to Robert D. Enright, Department of Educational Psychology, University of Wisconsin–Madison, 1025 W. Johnson Street, Madison, WI 53706. E-mail: forgive@sbcglobal.net

MANY CHILDREN IN AMERICA'S central cities are exposed to at least three factors that put their ability to maintain internal and relational peace at risk: (a) poverty, (b) racism, and (c) exposure to violence. These factors increase the likelihood that a child will experience problems in regulating emotional states such as depression, anxiety, and anger. Moreover, over time these negative emotions can give rise to psychological disorders and an inclination toward interpersonal violence in some children. Recent research shows that forgiveness can be an antidote to these negative experiences, especially excessive anger (Baskin & Enright, 2004; Enright & Fitzgibbons, 2000). Based on such findings, we are designing and implementing a forgiveness education program in Milwaukee's inner city.[1]

Inner-City America and Children's Emotional and Moral Development

The Effect of Poverty

Not surprisingly, growing up in a family that experiences chronic financial need is deleterious to children's development. In general, data demonstrate that poor children have more mental health problems than children who are not poor, regardless of whether we consider internalizing problems (such as anxiety or depression) or externalizing problems (such as antisocial behavior). These disadvantages increase in proportion to the amount of time a child spends in poverty (Bolger, Patterson, Thompson, & Kupersmidt, 1995; Duncan, Brooks-Gunn, & Khlebanov, 1994; McLeod & Shanahan, 1993; Samaan, 2000). Analysis of a large, longitudinal database demonstrated that past and current poverty levels are positively associated with levels of depression and antisocial behavior in children (McLeod & Shanahan, 1996). In this study, number of years in poverty was positively related to increases in antisocial behavior over the late 1980s and early 1990s. Longitudinal research in Australia has suggested that poverty experienced in the first 5 years of life negatively affects the mental health of the young person even as late as adolescence (Spence, Najman, Bor, O'Callaghan, & Williams, 2002), whereas recent experimental work shows that children—especially boys—remaining in impoverished neighborhoods have worse mental health and academic outcomes than those who have been moved to more affluent areas (even if family income does not change; Leventhal & Brooks-Gunn, 2003, 2004).

The child raised in poverty is likely to be exposed to anger-producing interpersonal injury on several levels. First, by its nature, poverty creates a sense of injustice: The poor person has much less than one who is more affluent. Second, studies consistently indicate that parents living in poverty tend to be more depressed and display more negative parenting behaviors (e.g., rejection of child and excessive physical punishment; Brody & Flor, 1998; Brody, Murray, Kim, & Brown, 2002; Eamon, 2002); recent work has shown that mothers' psychological health and parenting skills are partial mediators of poverty's deleterious effect on children (Brody et al., 2002; Eamon, 2002). Therefore, it is likely that many poorer children struggle with issues of injustice committed within the family. Finally, living in poverty increases the likelihood of being exposed to criminal acts. Forgiveness can play a protective role in promoting children's resilience and commitment to living peaceful lives, in part by helping children cope with the anger that naturally arises in such situations.

The Effects of Racism

Another risk factor potentially affecting many inner-city children is the experience of racism. A variety of studies demonstrate the link between exposure to various forms of racism and mental health among adults (e.g., Fang & Myers, 2001; Williams & Williams-Morris, 2000). It is not surprising that Klonoff, Landrine, and Ullman (1999) reported that, of several different predictor variables, racial discrimination (a) was the best predictor of physical complaints, anxiety, and overall psychiatric symptom scores and (b) remained a significant predictor of other mental health variables after other predictor variables were controlled.

One might ask, however, if such relationships between exposure to racism and psychological well-being, established with adult participants, hold for children as well. Although there is not much work in this area, the tentative answer is yes. Simons et al. (2002) reported a moderate correlation ($r = .31$) between depressive symptomatology and personal experience of discrimination among a large sample of African American children. This relationship remained positive and significant when caretaker reports of discrimination were substituted for child reports. Reported prevalence of discrimination at the community level was also significantly related to depressive symptoms.

Nyborg and Curry (2003) provided a more detailed picture of the processes underlying the link between exposure to discrimination and mental health among ethnic minority youth. Their research with African American early adolescent males demonstrated that the relationship between experience of various forms of racism (personal and institutional) and various mental health outcomes (externalizing and internalizing symptoms as reported by self and parent and self-concept) was usually *fully* mediated by trait (pervasive, ongoing) anger. Research shows that forgiveness education is effective in reducing trait anger in particular (Gambaro, 2002).

The Effects of Exposure to Violence

The development of children is also threatened due to exposure to violence. Data from a subset of American cities show that 75%–90% of children in the inner-city have been exposed to or directly victimized by crime (Kuther & Wallace, 2003). Recent qualitative and quantitative reviews of psychological correlates of exposure to community violence have demonstrated that children who are exposed to—or in some cases only hear about—community violence are at risk for elevated levels of depression, anger, anxiety, sleep problems, behavior problems, and symptoms that parallel those of posttraumatic stress disorder (Garbarino, Dubrow, Kostelny, & Pardo, 1992; Johnson et al., 2002; Kupersmidt, Shahinfar, & Voegler-Lee, 2002). The link between victimization and depression has been established empirically among African American youths in particular (Fitzpatrick, 1993); other empirical work with this subgroup has suggested that negative coping skills mediate the relationship between violence and mental health (Dempsey, 2002). A recent review (Kuther & Wallace, 2003) made a strong case for the negative impact of direct and indirect exposure to violence on African American children's sociomoral development; the argument can probably be extended to children of other ethnic groups as well. Not surprisingly, academic problems are also common and may well be caused at least in part by the emotional consequences described earlier (Garbarino et al., 1992; Schwartz & Gorman, 2003).

The Importance of Targeting Anger

Given the multiplicity of injustices children in the inner city face, it is reasonable to assume that anger is a relatively common experience among them. Recent evidence suggests that anger interferes with adequate solution of the two main developmental tasks of childhood: establishing positive peer relationships (Sullivan, 1953) and achieving academically (Erikson, 1968). Anger is linked to aggression in general and, in particular, to reactive aggression (Arsenio, Cooperman, & Lover, 2000; Price & Dodge, 1989; Smith, Furlong, Bates, & Laughlin, 1998; Zeman, Shipman, & Suveg, 2002). Reactive aggression involves responding with hostility and defensiveness to another's behavior. It can be contrasted with proactive aggression, which is unprovoked and instrumental in nature. The data show that children who demonstrate reactive aggression are at risk for poor peer relationships and a variety of other social and psychological problems (Price & Dodge, 1989; Waschbusch, Willoughby, & Pelham, 1998); this is also true of children who are angry but not necessarily aggressive (Arsenio et al., 2000; Eisenberg, Pidada, & Liew, 2001; Fabes & Eisenberg, 1992). On the other hand, correlations between proactive aggression and peer status, or other indicators of adjustment, tend to be not significant or even positive (Waschbusch et al., 1998). Although less well documented, some evidence suggests that anger may be negatively related to learning and academic achievement (Boekaerts, 1994; Gambaro, 2002; Pekrun, Goetz, Titz, & Perry, 2002).

Our work in forgiveness education is based on the conviction that anger reduction is the fundamental salutary effect of forgiveness, and that a decrease in anger leads to less depression and anxiety and to stronger academic achievement and more peaceful social behavior. We propose this chain of events based on several sources of evidence. First, the thorough review by Enright and Fitzgibbons (2000) of empirical and clinical data on forgiveness and mental health concluded that anger reduction was the key component of the beneficial impact of forgiveness on mental health. Second, some correlational data show that children's problems with anger regulation predict internalizing symptoms better than difficulties with regulating sadness, suggesting that when the child experiences comorbid negative emotional states, anger may be primary (Zeman et al., 2002). These strands of evidence suggest that reduction of anger is critical to children's successful navigation of appropriate developmental tasks, including establishing positive relationships. The finding that middle childhood seems to be a critical time for learning to regulate anger (Brown, Covell, & Abramovitch, 1991; McCoy & Masters, 1985) makes forgiveness education in the schools especially appropriate.

Interpersonal Forgiveness

The concept of forgiveness. Our research group at the University of Wisconsin–Madison (UW–Madison) has pioneered work in the psychology of forgiveness over the past 18 years. Conceptually, forgiveness is defined as follows:

> People, on rationally determining that they have been unfairly treated, forgive when they willfully abandon resentment and related responses (to which they have a right) and endeavor to respond to the wrongdoer based on the moral principle of beneficence, which may include compassion, unconditional worth, generosity, and moral love (to which the wrongdoer, by nature of the hurtful act or acts, has no right). (Enright & Fitzgibbons, 2000, p. 29)

A definition more amenable to psychological study construes forgiveness as overcoming negative thoughts, feelings, and behaviors directed at an offender and developing positive thoughts, feelings, and behaviors vis-à-vis the same (Enright & the Human Development Study Group, 1991). Before beginning empirical work on the topic, our group thoroughly reviewed philosophical work on forgiveness, which makes clear that forgiveness is offered from a position of strength (Enright & the Human Development Study Group, 1991). Forgiveness does not make one weak or vulnerable; it should be confused neither with condoning (e.g., ignoring or subtly approving) an offense, nor with reconciliation (reestablishing a relationship with an offender). Forgiveness does not preclude *moderate, limited* expressions of anger or a search for *reasonable* redress of injustice. Because forgiveness is a specific personal response to injustice and because harmful reactions to injustice appear to be at the root of some unhealthy psychological and relational patterns, it follows that a forgiveness intervention should be appropriate in a context where such negative experiences prevail.

Our group's work demonstrates that the process of forgiveness can be broken down into 20 units (see Table 1). Individuals need not progress through all units in order but may flow between units as they forgive. These units can be generalized into the *uncovering phase* (admitting the fact of the offense and experiencing its negative consequences), the *decision phase* (feeling a need for change and deciding to forgive), the *work phase* (trying to see the offender through different eyes and with a softened heart), and the *deepening phase* (finding meaning and purpose in the offense and experiencing the benefits of forgiveness).

The concept of unconditionality. As elaborated later, our research group has developed a variety of interventions that assist people in forgiving offenders. One of the key social-cognitive processes in these interventions—including the one being implemented in Milwaukee—is what we term *unconditionality* (Enright & the Human Development Study Group, 1994). Unconditionality is the understanding that all persons are equal at some level, regardless of personal characteristics (e.g., skin color, socioeconomic status). This understanding is based on the Piagetian concept of identity: the intellectual understanding that $A + 0 = A$, or that something unessential added to the first value does not alter it. (Piaget's famous conservation tasks demonstrate this principle: Pouring water from a short, wide container to a tall, narrow container is the "0" component, whereas the volume of water is the "A" component.) Unconditionality arises from this basic cognitive skill of identity and then leads to a belief in the moral principle of inherent worth, the conviction that persons are in essence equal, despite varying psychological characteristics (including behavior). Offering forgiveness involves acting on this social-cognitive understanding and the moral principle of inherent worth that springs from it.

Table 1
The Phases and Units of Forgiveness (Enright & Fitzgibbons, 2000, p. 68)

Uncovering phase
  1. Examination of psychological defenses
  2. Confrontation of anger; the point being to release, not harbor, the anger
  3. Admittance of shame, when this is appropriate
  4. Awareness of depleted emotional energy
  5. Awareness of cognitive rehearsal
  6. Insight that the injured party may be comparing self with the injurer
  7. Realization that oneself may be permanently and adversely changed by the injury
  8. Insight into a possibly altered just world view

Decision phase
  9. A change of heart/conversion/new insights that old resolution strategies are not working
  10. Willingness to consider forgiveness as an option
  11. Commitment to forgive offender

Work phase
  12. Reframing, through role taking, who the wrongdoer is by viewing him or her in context
  13. Empathy and compassion toward the offender
  14. Bearing/accepting the pain
  15. Giving a moral gift to the offender

Deepening phase
  16. Finding meaning for self and others in the suffering and in the forgiveness process
  17. Realizing that self has needed others' forgiveness in the past
  18. Insight that one is not alone
  19. Realization that one may have a new purpose in life due to the injury
  20. Awareness of decreased negative affect and, perhaps, increased positive affect, if this begins to emerge toward the injurer; awareness of internal, emotional release

Note. The material in this table is explained for the general public in Enright (2001).

Experimental research on forgiveness interventions. For 15 years, our group has been designing forgiveness interventions for use with various populations. Interventions implemented with such groups as survivors of sexual abuse (Freedman & Enright, 1996), college students in conflict with parents (Al-Mabuk, Enright, & Cardis, 1995; Lin, 1998), substance abusers (Lin, Mack, Enright, Krahn, & Baskin., 2004), mentally ill criminals (Chapman et al., 2001), and terminal cancer patients (Hansen, 2002) demonstrate that forgiveness interventions typically decrease negative psychological experiences such as depression and anger and increase positive psychological characteristics such as hope and self-esteem. A recent meta-analysis (Baskin & Enright, 2004) showed that the average effect size on mental health measures for such interventions implemented with groups is .59 of a standard deviation, and for those implemented with individuals—1.42 of a standard deviation.

More recently, scholars in our group have been implementing forgiveness programs with young adolescents. Gambaro (2002) found that forgiveness intervention with especially angry adolescents was more effective than a Rogerian-based support group in reducing various forms of anger and improving attitudes toward school and quality of interpersonal relationships. These findings were maintained at follow-up 9 months later, when Gambaro also assessed school grades and detentions. Students participating in the forgiveness intervention were significantly better on these measures as well. Park (2003) implemented a forgiveness curriculum in Korea with female adolescents who were aggressive victims of peer abuse and found that intervention participants demonstrated less anger, delinquency, aggression, and hostile attributions than did participants in two control groups. Gains were maintained at a 6-week follow-up, when the intervention group also showed significantly more empathy than the others.

Pilot of forgiveness education in Belfast, Northern Ireland. The manual-based forgiveness intervention we are implementing in Milwaukee schools is also being piloted on a small scale in Belfast, Northern Ireland. During the 1st year of implementation, anger dropped significantly more in children in the experimental group than in children in the control condition. This effect was especially pronounced for children who were extremely angry at the outset of the project; these children also demonstrated less depression at posttest than their counterparts in the control group. In addition, program children demonstrated significantly greater increases than control children in prosocial touching behaviors (e.g., hugging) over the course of the intervention.

A Forgiveness Curriculum for Milwaukee

In this section, we describe the general content of our school-based intervention with students in Milwaukee. Our 1st year within 13 first-grade classrooms commenced in the 2004–2005 academic year. All of the classrooms were in alternative (private) schools within the central city. We randomized the classrooms to an experimental (forgiveness education) and control group (no forgiveness education) with pretest and posttest evaluations. Dependent measures include each child's level of forgiving someone who hurt them unjustly, levels of anger and depression, interaction patterns with other children in the school setting, and achievement and conduct information gleaned from school records.

Besides first grade, we plan to have forgiveness curricula in third grade, early middle school, and early high school. The point is to have increasingly more complex ideas about forgiveness introduced over the years so that, at the end of high school, the students will have an opportunity to deeply understand the concept of forgiveness and to make informed choices about its relevance within their own lives.

Throughout our manualized intervention for first-grade children, we are targeting a particular aspect of children's social-cognitive development: reframing (Unit 12 in Table 1), in which the child understands that all people, even those who are unfair, have worth. Through our manual, children are and will be taught about inherent worth of all people and to act on this insight by displaying the moral qualities of moral love (acting more out of a concern for the well-being of another than for oneself), kindness, respect, and/or generosity to those around them, including the ones who have hurt them. These five elements (reframing for inherent worth, moral love, kindness, respect, and generosity) are the focus of the first-grade program. In the program we are careful to emphasize the distinction between forgiveness and reconciliation. A child does not reconcile with an unrepentant bully, for example. These elements are key in the work phase of the model of forgiveness presented in Table 1, which has been the crux of all forgiveness interventions conducted to date.

To emphasize the aforementioned five elements, we have a three-part curriculum. The first part simply introduces these five concepts outside the context of forgiveness through the story-medium of Dr. Seuss's books. Part 2 introduces these five concepts again, but this time *within the context of forgiveness,* using stories again by Dr. Seuss. Part 3 introduces these five concepts within the context of the *child's own attempt to forgive someone.*

The third-grade manual will go into greater depth in linking the moral principle of beneficence to forgiveness, which will be illustrated through more advanced literature such as *The Velveteen Rabbit* (Williams, 1958) and *Rising Above the Storm Clouds* (Enright, 2004). The outlines for the middle school manual and beyond are still being developed and therefore are not discussed here.

Throughout the curriculum, the teachers make the important distinction between *learning* about forgiveness and *choosing to practice it* in certain contexts. Children are always free to try or not try forgiveness in response to their own personal hurts borne out of unfair treatment. In our experience in Belfast to date, children willingly try forgiveness when they are free to choose the person who was unfair to them and the event that each child considers to be unfair. The child's own classroom teacher delivers the curriculum. Prior to the commencement of the program, we hold a 1-day workshop for participating teachers in which we introduce them to the basic concepts of forgiveness, hand out the curriculum manuals, and discuss any questions or concerns. After the workshop, we are in close contact with each teacher through phone, e-mail, and visits to the school as needed. To us, it is important that the child's own teacher, rather than our research group, impart the concepts to the children to ensure cultural and religious sensitivity regarding the nuances of forgiveness.

Concluding Thoughts

Children in America's inner cities are faced with injustice on personal, institutional, and systemic levels. Anger arising from such experiences contributes to psychological and social conflict. Our forgiveness curriculum serves as *remediation* for children already suffering from excessive anger and its consequences and as *prevention* for all children against the development of further psychological and relational problems related to toxic levels of this emotion. As a result, children participating in forgiveness education should have the knowledge and skills to embody peace in their own lives and eventually to promote it within and between persons and communities.

Our vision is to give children in violent communities enough time to learn so deeply about forgiveness that it is as natural as breathing. Having learned well the process of forgiveness in childhood, these people as adults may be better equipped than their forebears to see the *enemy* as a genuine human being worthy of respect. Is true peace ever to be realized without such a perspective and ethical responses based on that perspective? Forgiveness within individuals' hearts and minds may change communities that have not known peace for many decades. In other words, forgiveness education, though it has immediate benefits of improved emotional health, may have even wider benefits as more psychologically healthy adults are able to sit down together for mutual benefit as well as gain to the entire community. Forgiveness has rarely been a part of the peace movement. Perhaps it is time to change that for the sake of the children and the future health of entire communities.

Note

1. Demographically, Milwaukee is a microcosm of U.S. at-risk populations. Milwaukee's 1999 poverty rate (21.3%) exceeds those of nearby major cities such as Chicago (19.6%) and Minneapolis (16.9%; Milwaukee Department of City Development, Long Range Planning Division, 2003, p. 140). This snapshot hides the marked deterioration the city has experienced over the past 30 years. The most recent longitudinal analyses have shown that Milwaukee's poverty rate nearly doubled from 1970 to 1990 (Levine, 1998). African American Milwaukeeans have been hit particularly hard: Their poverty rate is about two times the rate of European Americans (Levine, 1998). In fact, Black poverty rates are higher in Milwaukee than in any other city in the north central United States (Levine, 1998). Regarding racial issues, 18% of Milwaukee urban area residents identify themselves as African American, and 7% identify as Hispanic (U.S. Census Bureau, 2000). Other ethnic minorities and people of mixed ethnic background are also present but constitute a minimal percentage of the population. It is not unreasonable, therefore, to estimate that ethnic minorities constitute about 30% of the Milwaukee area population. Regarding community violence, crime statistics show that, between 2001 and 2002, arrests for violent offenses in the state of Wisconsin increased by 1.4% (Wisconsin Office of Justice Assistance, 2002), whereas the nearby city of Chicago saw a decrease of 1.6% in arrests for similar crimes over the same period (Index Crime in Chicago, 2003). Of course, not all criminal acts in Wisconsin are committed in Milwaukee, but the clear majority of some types of crimes are. For example, 149 of the 196 murders reported throughout Wisconsin in 2001 were committed in Milwaukee (Milwaukee Police Department annual report, 2001; Wisconsin Office of Justice Assistance, 2002).

References

Al-Mabuk, R. H., Enright, R. D., & Cardis, P. (1995). Forgiveness education with parentally love-deprived late adolescents. *Journal of Moral Education, 24*, 427–443.

Arsenio, W. F., Cooperman, S., & Lover, A. (2000). Affective predictors of preschoolers' aggression and peer acceptance: Direct and indirect effects. *Developmental Psychology, 36*, 438–448.

Baskin, T. W., & Enright, R. D. (2004). Intervention studies of forgiveness: A meta-analysis. *Journal of Counseling and Development, 82*, 79–90.

Boekaerts, M. (1994). Anger in relation to school learning. *Learning and Instruction, 3*, 269–280.

Bolger, K. E., Patterson, C. J., Thompson, W. W., & Kupersmidt, J. B. (1995). Psychosocial adjustment among children experiencing persistent and intermittent family economic hardship. *Child Development, 66*, 1107–1129.

Brody, G. H., & Flor, D. L. (1998). Maternal resources, parenting practices, and child competence in rural, single-parent African American families. *Child Development, 69*, 803–816.

Brody, G. H., Murray, V. M., Kim, S., & Brown, A. C. (2002). Longitudinal pathways to competence and psychological adjustment among African American children living in rural single-parent households. *Child Development, 73*, 1505–1516.

Brown, K., Covell, K., & Abramovitch, R. (1991). Time course and control of emotion: Age differences in understanding and recognition. *Merrill-Palmer Quarterly, 37*, 273–287.

Chapman, R. F., Maier, G., Owen, A., Nousse, V., Park, J. H., & Enright, R. D. (2001, July). *Healing forgiveness: Group cognitive therapy for abused male forensic patients.* Paper presented at the World Congress of Behavioral and Cognitive Therapies, Vancouver, Canada.

Dempsey, M. (2002). Negative coping as a mediator in the relation between violence and outcomes: Inner-city African-American youth. *American Journal of Orthopsychiatry, 72*, 102–109.

Duncan, G. J., Brooks-Gunn, J., & Khlebanov, P. K. (1994). Economic deprivation and early child development. *Child Development, 65*, 296–318.

Eamon, M. K. (2002). Influences and mediators of the effect of poverty on young adolescent depressive symptoms. *Journal of Youth and Adolescence, 31*, 231–242.

Eisenberg, N., Pidada, S., & Liew, J. (2001). The relations of regulation and negative emotionality to Indonesian children's social functioning. *Child Development, 72*, 1747–1763.

Enright, R. D. (2001). *Forgiveness is a choice: A step-by-step process for resolving anger and restoring hope.* Washington, DC: APA Life Tools.

Enright, R. D. (2004). *Rising above the storm clouds: What it's like to forgive.* Washington, DC: Magination.

Enright, R. D., & Fitzgibbons, R. P. (2000). *Helping clients forgive: An empirical guide for resolving anger and restoring hope.* Washington, DC: American Psychological Association.

Enright, R. D., & the Human Development Study Group. (1991). The moral development of forgiveness. In W. Kurtines & J. Gewirtz (Eds.), *Handbook of moral behavior and development*, Vol. 1 (pp. 123–152). Hillsdale, NJ: Lawrence Erlbaum Associates, Inc.

Enright, R. D., & the Human Development Study Group. (1994). Piaget on the moral development of forgiveness: Identity or reciprocity? *Human Development, 37*, 63–80.

Erikson, E. (1968). *Identity: Youth and crisis.* New York: Norton.

Fabes, R. A., & Eisenberg, N. (1992). Young children's coping with interpersonal anger. *Child Development, 63*, 116–128.

Fang, C. Y., & Myers, H. F. (2001). The effects of racial stressors and hostility on cardiovascular reactivity in African American and Caucasian Men. *Health Psychology, 20*, 64–70.

Fitzpatrick, K. M. (1993). Exposure to violence and presence of depression among low-income African-American youth. *Journal of Consulting and Clinical Psychology, 61*, 528–531.

Freedman, S. R., & Enright, R. D. (1996). Forgiveness as an intervention goal with incest survivors. *Journal of Counseling and Clinical Psychology, 64*, 983–992.

Gambaro, M. E. (2002). *School-based forgiveness education in the management of trait anger in early adolescents.* Unpublished doctoral dissertation, University of Wisconsin–Madison.

Garbarino, J., Dubrow, N., Kostelny, K., & Pardo, C. (1992). *Children in danger: Coping with the consequences of community violence.* San Francisco, CA: Jossey-Bass.

Hansen, M. J. (2002). *Forgiveness as an educational intervention goal for persons at the end of life.* Unpublished doctoral dissertation, University of Wisconsin–Madison.

Index crime in Chicago: Year-end 2002. (2003). Retrieved September 17, 2003, from http://egov.

cityofchicago.org/webportal/COCWebPortal/COC_EDITORIAL/Index02End.pdf

Johnson, R. M., Kotch, J. B., Catellier, D. J., Winsor, J. R., Dufort, V., Hunter, W., et al. (2002). Adverse behavioral and emotional outcomes from child abuse and witnessed violence. *Child Maltreatment, 7,* 179–186.

Klonoff, E. A., Landrine, H., & Ullman, J. B. (1999). Racial discrimination and psychiatric symptoms among Blacks. *Cultural Diversity and Ethnic Minority Psychology, 5,* 329–339.

Kupersmidt, J. B., Shahinfar, A., & Voegler-Lee, M. E. (2002). Children's exposure to community violence. In A. M. LaGreca, W. K. Silverman, E. M. Vernberg, & M. C. Roberts (Eds.), *Helping children cope with disasters and terrorism* (pp. 381–401). Washington, DC: American Psychological Association.

Kuther, T. L., & Wallace, S. C. (2003). Community violence and sociomoral development: An African American cultural perspective. *Journal of Orthopsychiatry, 73,* 177–189.

Leventhal, T., & Brooks-Gunn, J. (2003). Moving to opportunity: An experimental study of neighborhood effects on mental health. *American Journal of Public Health, 93,* 1576–1582.

Leventhal, T., & Brooks-Gunn, J. (2004). A randomized study of neighborhood effects on low-income children's educational outcomes. *Developmental Psychology, 40,* 488–507.

Levine, M. V. (with Callaghan, S. J.). (1998). *The economic status of Milwaukee: The city and the region, May, 1998.* Retrieved September 17, 2003, from http://www.uwm.edu/Dept/CED/publications/milw98.html

Lin, W. F., Mack, D., Enright, R. D., Krahn, D., & Baskin, T. (2004). Effects of forgiveness therapy on anger, mood, and vulnerability to substance use among inpatient substance-dependent clients. *Journal of Consulting and Clinical Psychology, 72,* 1114–1121.

Lin, W. N. (1998). *Forgiveness as an intervention goal with late adolescents with insecure attachment in Taiwan.* Unpublished doctoral dissertation, University of Wisconsin–Madison.

McCoy, C. L., & Masters, J. C. (1985). The development of children's strategies for the social control of emotion. *Child Development, 56,* 1214–1222.

McLeod, J. D., & Shanahan, M. J. (1993). Poverty, parenting, and children's mental health. *American Sociological Review, 58,* 351–366.

McLeod, J. D., & Shanahan, M. J. (1996). Trajectories of poverty and children's mental health. *Journal of Health and Social Behavior, 37,* 207–220.

Milwaukee Department of City Development, Long Range Planning Division. (2003). *2000 city of Milwaukee urban atlas: Summary of population and housing characteristics based on the 2000 U.S. Census.* Milwaukee, WI: Author.

Milwaukee Police Department annual report. (2001). Retrieved September 17, 2003, from http://www.milwaukeepolice.org/2001AnnualReport.pdf

Nyborg, V. M., & Curry, J. F. (2003). The impact of perceived racism: Psychological symptoms among African American boys. *Journal of Clinical Child and Adolescent Psychology, 32,* 258–266.

Park, J. H. (2003). *Validating a forgiveness education program for adolescent female aggressive victims in Korea.* Unpublished doctoral dissertation, University of Wisconsin–Madison.

Pekrun, R., Goetz, T., Titz, W., & Perry, R. P. (2002). Academic emotions in students' self-regulated learning and achievement: A program of qualitative and quantitative research. *Educational Psychologist, 37,* 91–105.

Price, J. M., & Dodge, K. A. (1989). Reactive and proactive aggression in childhood: Relations to peer status and social context dimension. *Journal of Abnormal Child Psychology, 17,* 455–471.

Samaan, R. A. (2000). The influence of race, ethnicity, and poverty on the mental health of children. *Journal of Health Care for the Poor and Underserved, 11,* 100–110.

Schwartz, D., & Gorman, A. H. (2003). Community violence exposure and children's academic functioning. *Journal of Educational Psychology, 95,* 163–173.

Simons, R. L., Murray, V., McLoyd, V., Lin, K., Cutrona, C., & Conger, R. D. (2002). Discrimination, crime, ethnic identity, and parenting as correlates of depressive symptoms among African American children: A multilevel analysis. *Development and Psychopathology, 14,* 371–393.

Smith, D. C., Furlong, M. J., Bates, M., & Laughlin, J. D. (1998). Development of the multi-dimensional school anger inventory for males. *Psychology in the Schools, 35,* 1–15.

Spence, S. H., Najman, J. M., Bor, W., O'Callaghan, M., & Williams, G. M. (2002). Maternal anxiety and depression, poverty, and marital relationship factors during early childhood as predictors of anxiety and depressive symptoms in adolescence. *Journal of Child Psychology and Psychiatry, 43,* 459–469.

Sullivan, H. S. (1953). *The interpersonal theory of psychiatry.* New York: Norton.

U.S. Census Bureau. (2000). *Detailed tables: Hispanic or Latino, and not Hispanic or Latino by race: Total population*. Retrieved September 23, 2003, from http://factfinder.census.gov/servlet/DTTable?_ts=82371290655

Waschbusch, D. A., Willoughby, M. T., & Pelham, W. E. (1998). Criterion validity and the utility of reactive and proactive aggression: Comparisons to attention deficit hyperactivity disorder, oppositional defiant disorder, conduct disorder, and other measures of functioning. *Journal of Clinical Child Psychology, 4,* 396–405.

Williams, D. R., & Williams-Morris, R. (2000). Racism and mental health: The African American experience. *Ethnicity and Health, 5,* 243–268.

Williams, M. (1958). *The velveteen rabbit*. New York: Doubleday.

Wisconsin Office of Justice Assistance. (2002). *Preliminary state-wide crime and arrests in Wisconsin—2002*. Retrieved September 17, 2003, from http://oja.state.wi.us/asx/crime2002.asp

Zeman, J., Shipman, K., & Suveg, C. (2002). Anger and sadness regulation: Predictions to internalizing and externalizing symptoms in children. *Journal of Clinical Child and Adolescent Psychology, 31,* 393–398.

Jodie Lodge
Erica Frydenberg

The Role of Peer Bystanders in School Bullying: Positive Steps Toward Promoting Peaceful Schools

Bullying and harassment are pervasive problems in schools, with interventions to counter bullying now regarded as a matter of high priority by educational authorities. This article considers the impact of bullying on victim and bully. It also explores the role of peers as bystanders in school bullying. Australian research is described, examining peer perceptions and responses, together with factors associated with bystander behavior. The authors' research suggests that teaching peers to cope may go some way to combating bullying in school by effecting change at the peer group level. Features of a universal coping program are given and common elements of successful antibullying interventions are highlighted. It is clear that peers play a central role in school bullying and teaching young people strategies to cope may be a positive step toward promoting peaceful schools.

Jodie Lodge is a Doctor in Educational Psychology and Research Associate at The University of Melbourne. Erica Frydenberg is an Associate Professor in the Department of Learning and Educational Development at the University of Melbourne.

Correspondence should be addressed to Jodie Lodge, Department of Learning and Educational Development, Level 3, 234 Queensberry Street, University of Melbourne, Carlton, Victoria, 3010, Australia. E-mail: lodge@unimelb.edu.au

THE RIGHT TO BE EDUCATED without suffering from victimization has resonated with the wider public, especially after the tragic school shootings at Columbine High School in Littleton, Colorado, in 1999, and Santana High School in Santee, California, in early 2001. Research on the 37 school shootings that took place in North America between 1974 and 2000, including Columbine, found that 71% of the attackers felt persecuted, bullied, threatened, attacked, or injured by others prior to the incident. A number of the young attackers were frequently bullied and harassed by their peers, with one young attacker being described as "the kid everyone teased" (Secret Service & the U.S. Department of Education, 2002).

Bullying and harassment are pervasive problems in schools. Researchers estimate that 1.6 million school-aged young people in the United States are bullied at least once a week (Olweus & Limber, 1999). In Australia, it is estimated that one in six young people experience victimization at school (Rigby, 1997). Reports of being bullied are among the main reasons for young Australians to call the national Kids Help Line (2002).

In Australia, as elsewhere, school bullying is now widely regarded as a distinct form of aggressive behavior and not simply the outcome of individual differences (Rigby, 1997). In recent years, the social context in which bullying occurs has become increasingly salient in the literature, particularly the role of peers in reinforcing bullying episodes. In this article we examine the likelihood of peer responses to bullying. We discuss factors related to supporting victims of bullying and ways of teaching peers to cope so that they can contribute to a safe and peaceful learning environment.

The Nature of School Bullying

Bullying in schools is frequently defined in terms of power, intent to harm, and frequency (Rigby, 1996). For those who bully there is power, either physical or through peer group status. For the bullied young person, the acts are deliberate, causing physical, psychological, and emotional harm. Bullying is not random, and victims live with the fear of further attacks. Bullying in schools is not limited to physical assaults, but also includes verbal abuse, harassment, threats, and intimidation—with verbal bullying the most common form of aggression experienced by school-aged young people (Patton et al., 1998). Reported victimization is typically directed at the young person due to ethnicity, resistance to conform to pressure from peers, physical differences, high achievement, being new to the school, sexual orientation, and socioeconomic background (Kids Help Line, 2002).

The Impact

There are harmful effects on victims and perpetrators of bullying. Victimization impacts significantly on young peoples' ability to learn, as well as their school attendance (Rigby, 1998). Findings confirm that victimization is clearly connected to low self-esteem, proneness to depression, maladjustment, low levels of well-being, and suicidal ideation (Besag, 1989; Craig, 1998; Rigby, 1998). Young people who are bullied tend to be withdrawn and anxious, and are typically characterized by tenseness, fears, and worries (Neary & Joseph, 1994). Those who are frequently harassed experience higher levels of distress and tend to feel more ashamed than their same age peers. They are also more inclined to retaliate when angered or provoked (Lodge, 2004).

Perpetrators of bullying are at high risk of maladjustment. Bullying other students is recognized as a risk factor for antisocial and criminal behavior (National Crime Prevention, 1999). Bullies are less likely to complete school, more likely to use drugs and alcohol, and more likely to engage in delinquent behaviors (Gottfredson, Gottfredson, & Hybl, 1993). There is evidence from longitudinal studies that aggressive and dominating behaviors are likely to continue over time (Pepler & Rubin, 1991; Tremblay, McCord, & Boileau, 1992). Findings from a Swedish study revealed that 60% of boys who were identified as bullies at age 13 to 16 had at least one criminal conviction by the age of 24 (Olweus, 1994). In Australia, boys who bullied others were more inclined to endorse domestic violence (Rigby, Whish, & Black, 1994). This evidence has been recognized in Australia, with early intervention for domestic violence focusing primarily on the prevention of school violence (Commonwealth of Australia, 2003).

Peer Involvement in Bullying

Peers witness bullying episodes at school. Canadian studies report that peers (bystanders) are present in as many as 85% of school bullying episodes (Craig, Pepler, & Atlas, 2000). Through their behavior in these situations, peers can affect the outcome of the episodes. Peer bystanders can encourage and prolong the bullying by providing attention or actually joining in with the harassment (Craig & Pepler, 1995). In a study of playground bullying, peers were found to spend 54% of their time reinforcing bullies by passively watching, 21% of their time actively modeling bullies, and 25% of their time intervening on behalf of victims (O'Connell, Pepler, & Craig, 1999). There are a variety of bystanding roles—behaviors that can be adopted by young people. Finnish research has identified these various participatory roles as supporting (cheering), joining in, passively watching, and occasionally intervening (Salmivalli, Lagerspetz, Bjorkqvist, Osterman, & Kaukiainen, 1996). Seen from this point of view, encouraging antibullying behaviors in peers could hold the greatest potential for intervention. However, a greater understanding of peer processes in bullying, together with an understanding of how bystanders cope, is needed.

The Concept of Coping

Coping is the behavioral and cognitive efforts that individuals use to meet the demands of their everyday situations. It includes the thoughts, feelings, and actions they use in response to the environment. Though there are theoretically an infinite number of ways an individual can cope, the possible responses have been empirically grouped to capture the construct. We know, for instance, that there are productive ways of coping, such as focusing on solving the problem, working hard to achieve, and focusing on the positive side of things. In contrast, there are nonproductive ways of coping, such as keeping things to oneself, blaming oneself, ignoring the problem, and worrying.

There is a great deal that we know about coping. We know that students who use productive coping strategies have a greater sense of well-being and those who use nonproductive strategies are likely to feel less comfortable about themselves and their circumstances (Frydenberg & Lewis, 2002). For example, in most circumstances students who use self-blame are likely to have a lesser sense of well-being. Productive coping is also associated with academic achievement. Students who use productive strategies are likely to achieve better than would be expected on the basis of ability alone (Frydenberg & Lewis, 1999). We also know that strategies that utilize the support of others, such as social support, can be most helpful in some circumstances.

Perceptions and Responses of Australian Bystanders

Our research has examined peer perceptions and responses to school bullying using hypothetical vignettes depicting verbal harassment of a student. We were interested in how students thought they would respond as bystanders and how their relationship to the bully and victim influenced their likelihood to respond. We were also interested in information on friendship quality, social-emotional adjustment, and coping. Three hypothetical verbal bullying vignettes, which included a weight insult, a clothing insult, and a peer rejection insult, were used to obtain data. Self-report information was obtained using The Friendship Scale (Rubenstein & Rubin, 1987), The Weinberger Adjustment Inventory–Short Form (Weinberger, Feldman, Ford, & Chastain, 1987), and The Children's Coping Scale–Short Form (CCS–SF adapted from the Adolescent Coping Scale–Short Form, Frydenberg & Lewis, 1993). Three hundred and seventy-nine students (185 girls and 194 boys), aged 10–13 years, from nine schools in metropolitan Melbourne, Australia, participated in the study. Fifty students also provided qualitative data about their own experiences of witnessing bullying. All parents gave informed consent, while students gave assent prior to their participation in the study.

Peer Participation in Verbal Bullying at School

Given that the responses to all three verbal bullying scenarios were quite similar, students' estimates (on a 4-point scale) on the likelihood of participating were summed to provide a general indicator of the probability of such a response. Analyses from this study (see Lodge & Frydenberg, 2004) revealed that the combined likelihood of participating was significantly related to gender. Though most students indicated that they would either not get involved (passively watch) or would support the target of the bullying, girls were significantly more likely to provide support for the victim, boys to support the bully. There was also a tendency for more girls than boys to report that they would not get involved. Although relatively few students indicated that they would join in with the bully, boys more commonly endorsed this response.

Factors Associated With Peer Participation

Our investigation revealed that there was a relationship between the likelihood of peers participating in verbal bullying and several characteristics associated with young people's friendships, adjustment, and coping. These characteristics are summarized in Table 1. For example, characteristics related to providing support for the victim included friendship, use of a productive style of coping, self-esteem, altruistic actions and feelings, the ability to avoid retaliation when angered, and high emotional support from friends.

Overall, the interpersonal relationship between the victim–perpetrator and the bystander was an important factor in participants' behavioral judgments when witnessing verbal bullying in school. Of note, the profiles of passive bystanders suggest that they do not feel affiliated with either the victim or bully and experience less emotional distress and apprehension (fear, guilt, helplessness) when witness to peer attacks. This has important implications for intervention work, as observational research confirms that young people who do nothing reinforce bullying by passively watching and not helping the victim (O'Connell et al., 1999). Passive observations by the majority inadvertently reinforce bullying and send a positive message to the bullies.

Coping actions were also related to bystander behavior. More notably, it would appear that those who use a productive style of coping are in a better position to provide support to victims of bullying by actively defending. However, it was also clear from the findings that witnessing verbal aggression evokes strong emotional responses from bystanders.

How Do Peers Feel About Bullying?

On the whole, bystanders expressed disgust and anger toward verbal harassment of peers. Girls were more likely to feel sad, upset, angry, and disgusted; boys were more likely to feel indifferent to witnessing verbal bullying. As bystanders, many young people reported conflicting feelings, including guilt, anger, confusion, lack of knowledge regarding what to do, and fear of becoming the next victim. In contrast, there were positive responses that indicated that young people felt good about having intervened. To illustrate the themes expressed, selections of responses are described in Table 2.

Table 1
Characteristics Related to the Likelihood of Peer Participation in Verbal Bullying

Factors Related to Supporting the Bully (i.e., Laugh & Cheer)	Factors Related to Joining in With the Bullying	Factors Related to Providing Support for the Victim (Defending)	Factors Related to Passively Watching (Not Get Involved)
Is a friend of the bully	Has low self-esteem	Is a friend of the victim	Is a neutral acquaintance
Has low self-esteem	Is low in emotional support from friends	Uses a productive style of coping	Is high in self-restraint
Is low in emotional support from friends		Has self-esteem	
Is high in friendship stress/ social dissatisfaction	Expresses fewer altruistic actions and feelings	Expresses more altruistic actions and feelings	
Is low in self-restraint	Is low in self-restraint	Is high in emotional support from friends	
Use fewer productive coping strategies			

Table 2
Themes Expressed by Bystanders

Theme	Student Comments
Unsuccessful intervening	They were pointing, laughing, and calling her names. I tried talking to them and telling them to stop, but they wouldn't.
	We asked him not to tease my friend, but he refused.
Retaliation	We stuck up for him [the friend] and got into a quick fight—we taught him [the bully] a lesson.
	I'll sort it out or I will get back at the person who did it to my friend.
Reluctance to become involved	I didn't say anything because I thought that the teaser would start picking on me.
	They pick on other people and when I tell them to stop, they turn on me.
	No one else stuck up for her. If someone else had stuck up for her, I would have stuck up for her as well.
	I think it is very nasty, but I'm too afraid to stand up for the boy because they might say I like him. I don't know what to do.
Emotional impact	I felt guilty when I saw how upset the girl looked.
	I feel bad because I didn't help him or call a teacher.
	I sometimes feel mad or angry.
	I feel good about myself. I stand up for my friends in trouble. I'll sort it out. My friends are part of me.

Our data illustrates the indeterminate nature of peer participation in bullying. Though young people expressed disgust and anger toward the harassment of peers and indicated support for the victim, they were also likely to not do anything (i.e., passively watch). There may be a variety of reasons why peers do not become involved. For example, participants in the study reflected concern over becoming the next victim—*I didn't say anything because I thought that the teaser would start picking on me*. This would seem to be a very real risk for bystanders, as the use of hostile strategies could potentially elicit a counter attack. Lack of confidence to intervene without the support of others was also noted—*No one else stuck up for her. If someone else had stuck up for her, I would have stuck up for her as well*. This corresponds with our questionnaire data, which identified emotional support from friends as a factor related to the likelihood that peers would support the victim. Peers may also lack strategies to intervene effectively. Examples include unsuccessful attempts to intervene (*I tried talking to them and telling them to stop, but they wouldn't*) and incidences of retaliation (*I will get back at the person who did* it). Taken together, it would appear that teaching young people strategies to use when they witness bullying would be a positive step in promoting peaceful interventions that effect change at the peer group level.

Teaching Bystanders to Cope

We know that coping strategies can be taught (Frydenberg, 2004). Teaching bystanders to cope may be one way of promoting peer support against bullying, given that young people who employ a productive style of coping at school are less inclined to support the bully and are likely to be more available for the bullied student. Peer support and mediation approaches to bullying are being taken up by an increasing number of schools, with evidence that the existence of peer support systems can encourage the seeking-help strategy (Naylor, Cowie, & del Rey, 2001).

One way of facilitating adaptive ways of coping is through universal school programs that target skill development for all young people. A program that has been evaluated in a number of school settings in and outside Australia is *The Best of Coping* (Frydenberg & Brandon, 2002). Developed for adolescents, the program provides a framework and language that allows young people to reflect on their current coping practices and make changes. Topics addressed include optimistic thinking, effective communication skills, effective problem solving, decision making, goal setting, and time management. There is also a session dedicated to looking at strategies that are not helpful and ways of finding alternative strategies.

Introducing programs into the school setting allows students to explore and develop an understanding of their own and alternative coping behaviors in a safe and supportive environment. Evaluations of the Best of Coping program reveal that there are benefits in teaching adolescents cognitive-based coping skills (Frydenberg et al., 2004). Relevant to this article, evaluation studies reveal that self-efficacy increases in students who participate in the universal coping program (Bugalski & Frydenberg, 2000; Cotta, Frydenberg, & Poole, 2001). Students with higher levels of self-efficacy would be expected to use a more productive style of coping and be more inclined to support the victim of bullying rather than the bully. An evaluation study with Australian adolescent girls found evidence for an increased usage of productive coping strategies postprogram, using hypothetical bullying scenarios (Tollit, 2002). In a similar vein, an evaluation study conducted in Northern Italy found that increases in problem solving skills postprogram were particularly useful for managing conflicts (Ferrari, Nota, Soresi, & Frydenberg, 2003).

Antibullying Interventions

Interventions to counter bullying in schools are now regarded as a matter of high priority by educational authorities. Intervention studies have been carried out around the world: United States, Norway, Great Britain, Germany, Belgium, Spain, Finland, Ireland, Austria, Switzerland, and Australia. The success rates of these large-scale intervention studies vary considerably. Olweus (1994) reported up to 50% reductions in bullying in Norwegian schools using a nationwide campaign. However, more modest results were achieved when replicated in the United States, Germany, and Belgium (Smith, Ananiadou, & Cowie, 2003). Other intervention projects report effect sizes that range from 15% (Smith & Sharp, 1994) to 30% reductions (Pepler, Craig, Ziegler, & Charach, 1994). Some report increases in bullying, possibly due to an increased awareness of bullying behavior (Soutter & McKenzie, 2000). Various factors may account for differences in the success of antibullying interventions. A meta-evaluation commissioned by the Australian Commonwealth Attorney-General's Department (Rigby, 2002) highlights some of the common elements in successful interventions, which may be used to inform good practice.

1. Interventions were more successful when implemented in the early years of schooling than in secondary school.
2. Intervention was better than no intervention (i.e., greater increases in bullying were noted in control groups who did not receive antibullying initiatives).
3. Level of school commitment and staff involvement influenced the success of interventions.

Conclusion

Clearly, more attention is needed to understand peer group processes involved in school bullying. Our research illustrates the indeterminate nature of peer participation in verbal bullying. Though peers expressed feelings of disgust and anger at witnessing verbal harassment of others and also endorsed support for the victim, they were also inclined to not get involved by passively watching. There are likely to be several reasons for students not to become involved, including a fear of becoming the next victim, a lack of confidence to intervene, and not having effective strategies. Our data confirm that peers who used a productive style of coping at school were more inclined to support the victim and less inclined to support the bully. It is suggested that teaching peers to cope may go some way in combating bullying in school by effecting change at the peer group level.

It is noted, however, that interventions targeting peer processes need to be promoted in the context of a whole-school, antibullying initiative. Actions need to occur at all levels of the school community (including students, staff, and parents) and across all school activities. This approach provides young people with the confidence that all members of their school community support these strategies. A systemic process is needed when intervening to counter bullying. Consideration should be given to relationships, roles, interactions, and communication within the system.

Though the task of devising more consistently effective antibullying interventions remains, it is clear that the chances of success are greater if interventions are carried out during the early years of schooling. Thus, there is a real need to develop and evaluate preventative programs that target bullying during these formative years, especially universal programs that include all students. Peers play a central role in the maintenance and course of school bullying. Teaching young people strategies to use when they witness bullying is a positive step toward promoting peaceful schools.

References

Besag, V. E. (1989). *Bullies and victims in schools*. Milton Keynes, UK: Open University Press.

Bugalski, K., & Frydenberg, E. (2000). Promoting effective coping in adolescents 'at risk' of depression. *Australian Journal of Guidance & Counselling, 10*, 112–132.

Commonwealth of Australia. (2003). *No violence in schools—building healthy relationships for young people*. Evaluation Report. Canberra, Australia.

Cotta, A., Frydenberg, E., & Poole, C. (2001). Coping skills training for adolescents at school. *Australian Educational & Developmental Psychology, 17*, 103–116.

Craig, W. (1998). The relationship among bullying, victimisation, depression, anxiety, and aggression in elementary school children. *Personality and Individual Differences, 24*, 123–130.

Craig, W., & Pepler, D. (1995). Peer processes in bullying and victimization: An observational study. *Exceptionality Education Canada, 5*, 81–95.

Craig, W. M., Pepler, D., & Atlas, R. (2000). Observations of *bullying* in the playground and in the classroom. *School Psychology International, 21*, 22–36.

Ferrari, L., Nota, L., Soresi, S., & Frydenberg, E. (2003). *The best of coping: A training to improve coping strategies*. Unpublished manuscript, University of Padua, Italy.

Frydenberg, E. (2004). Coping competences: What to teach and when. *Theory Into Practice, 43*, 14–22.

Frydenberg, E., & Brandon, C. M. (2002). *The best of coping*. Melbourne, Australia: Oz Child.

Frydenberg, E., & Lewis, R. (1993). *Manual: The Adolescent Coping Scale*. Melbourne, Australia: Australian Council for Educational Research.

Frydenberg, E., & Lewis, R. (1999). Academic and general wellbeing: The relationship with coping. *Australian Journal of Guidance and Counselling, 9*, 19–36.

Frydenberg, E., & Lewis, R. (2002). Adolescent well-being: Building young people's resources. In E. Frydenberg (Ed.), *Beyond coping: Meeting goals, visions, and challenges* (pp. 175–194). London: Oxford University Press.

Frydenberg, E., Lewis, R., Bugalski, K., Cotta, A., McCarthy, C., Luscombe-Smith, N., et al. (2004). Prevention is better than cure. *Educational Psychology in Practice, 20*, 117–133.

Gottfredson, D. C., Gottfredson, G., & Hybl, L. (1993). Managing adolescent behavior: A multiyear, multischool study. *American Educational Research Journal, 30*, 179–215.

Kids Help Line. (2002). *Bullying*. Brisbane, Australia: Kids Help Line. Retrieved March 9, 2005, from www.kidshelp.com.au

Lodge, J. (2004). *Coping with school bullying among young Australian adolescents*. Paper presented at the 25th Stress and Anxiety Research Society conference, Amsterdam, Netherlands.

Lodge, J., & Frydenberg, E. (2004). *Reaching out in friendship: The role of peer bystanders in school bullying*. Paper presented at the Australian Association for Research in Education conference, Melbourne, Australia.

National Crime Prevention. (1999). *Pathways to prevention: Developmental and early intervention approaches to crime in Australia*. Attorney-General's Department: Canberra, Australia.

Naylor, P., Cowie, H., & del Rey, R. (2001). Coping strategies of secondary school children in response to being bullied. *Child Psychology & Psychiatry Review, 6,* 114–120.

Neary, A., & Joseph, S. (1994). Peer victimization and its relationship to self-concept and depression among school girls. *Personality and Individual Differences, 16,* 183–186.

O'Connell, P., Pepler, D. J., & Craig, W. (1999). Peer involvement in bullying: Insights and challenges for intervention. *Journal of Adolescence, 22,* 437–452.

Olweus, D. (1994). Bullying at school: Long term outcomes for the victims and an effective school based intervention program. In R. Huesmann (Ed.), *Aggressive behavior. Current perspectives* (pp. 97–130). New York: Plenum.

Olweus, D., & Limber, S. (1999). *Blueprints for violence prevention: Bullying prevention program (book nine).* Boulder: University of Colorado at Boulder, Institute of Behavioral Science, Center for the Study and Prevention of Violence.

Patton, G., Glover, S., Bond, L., Butler, H., Godfrey, C., Di Pietro, G., et al. (1998). The Gatehouse Project: A systematic approach to mental health promotion in secondary schools. *Australian & New Zealand Journal of Psychiatry, 32,* 586–593.

Pepler, D. J., Craig, W., Ziegler, S., & Charach, A. (1994). An evaluation of an antibullying intervention in Toronto schools. *Canadian Journal of Community Mental Health. Special Issue: Prevention: Focus on children and youth, 13,* 95–110.

Pepler, D. J., & Rubin, K. H. (1991). *The development and treatment of childhood aggression.* Hillsdale, NJ: Lawrence Erlbaum Associates, Inc.

Rigby, K. (1996). *Bullying in schools: What to do about it.* Melbourne, Australia: Australian Council for Educational Research.

Rigby, K. (1997). What children tell us about bullying in schools. *Children Australia, 22,* 28–34.

Rigby, K. (1998). The relationship between reported health and involvement in bully/victim problems among male and female secondary school students. *Journal of Health Psychology, 3,* 465–476.

Rigby, K. (2002). *A meta-evaluation of methods and approaches to reducing bullying in pre-schools and in early primary school in Australia.* Canberra, Australia: Commonwealth Attorney-General's Department.

Rigby, K., Whish, A., & Black, G. (1994, August). Implications of school children's peer relations for wife abuse in Australia. *Criminology Australia,* 8–12.

Rubenstein, J., & Rubin, C. (1987). *The Adolescent Friendship Inventory.* Unpublished manuscript, Boston University Medical School.

Salmivalli, C., Lagerspetz, K., Bjorkqvist, K., Osterman, K., & Kaukiainen, A. (1996). Bullying as a group process: Participant roles and their relations to social status within the group. *Aggressive Behavior, 22,* 1–15.

Secret Service & United States Department Of Education. (2002). *The final report and findings of the safe school initiative: Implications for the prevention of school attacks in the United States.* Washington, DC. Retrieved March 9, 2005, from http://www.secretservice.gov/

Smith P., Ananiadou, K., & Cowie, H. (2003). Interventions to reduce school bullying. *Canadian Journal of Psychiatry, 48,* 591–599.

Smith, P. K., & Sharp, S. (Eds.). (1994). *School bullying: Insights and perspectives.* London: Routledge.

Soutter, A., & McKenzie, A. (2000). The use and effects of antibullying and anti-harrassment policies in Australian schools. *School Psychology International. Special Issue: Bullies and Victims, 21,* 96–105.

Tollit, M. (2002). *Assessing the effectiveness of The Best of Coping program with female adolescent students.* Unpublished dissertation, University of Melbourne, Australia.

Tremblay, R. E., McCord, J., & Boileau, H. (1992). Early disruptive behavior, poor school achievement, delinquent behavior and delinquent personality: A longitudinal analysis. *Journal of Consult Clinical Psychology, 6,* 64–72.

Weinberger, D. A., Feldman, S. S., Ford, M. E., & Chastain, R. L. (1987). *Construct validation of the Weinberger Adjustment Inventory.* Unpublished manuscript.

Ulrike Niens
Ed Cairns

Conflict, Contact, and Education in Northern Ireland

This article outlines educational responses to the conflict in Northern Ireland designed to promote intergroup harmony. Current research about the impact of these programs on children and young people is also reviewed to draw conclusions for practitioners in formal and informal educational settings who want to use intergroup contact to implement education for peace in the most effective way. The contact hypothesis has provided the theoretical framework for the majority of educational initiatives in Northern Ireland designed to promote peace, and it is used here to evaluate empirical evidence regarding the impact of such initiatives. In the main this evidence supports the importance of the key conditions for successful outgroup contact as originally proposed by the contact hypothesis. In addition, intergroup anxiety is identified as a factor mediating successful

Ulrike Niens is a UNESCO Centre Research Fellow in the School of Education at the University of Ulster. Ed Cairns is a Professor of Psychology at the University of Ulster.

Correspondence should be addressed to Ulrike Niens, UNESCO Centre, School of Education, University of Ulster, Room B102A, Coleraine Campus, Cromore Road, Coleraine, N. Ireland, BT52 1SA. E-mail: ucp.niens@ulster.ac.uk

outgroup contact and attention is drawn to the potentially significant role of outgroup contact that is not experienced first hand, but indirectly through reports of relevant others.

NORTHERN IRELAND IS A DIVIDED society and this is especially true where schooling is concerned with over 90% of children attending either a Catholic or a Protestant school at elementary and secondary level. From the early 1970s, educational research in Northern Ireland indicated potentially harmful effects of denominational segregation as possibly perpetuating negative intergroup attitudes and, ultimately, conflict (Abbott, Dunn, & Morgan, 1998; Cairns, 1987; Darby et al., 1977). Today it is widely accepted that segregation is not the cause of intergroup conflict, but it is believed to play a major role in establishing and maintaining conflict between two communities (Gallagher, 1995). As a result, policies and methods to reduce the level of segregation and to increase opportunities for intergroup contact have been introduced. The importance of this policy can be gauged by the fact that the government has spent millions of dollars in an attempt to improve intergroup relations (Knox & Hughes, 1996). In particular, the educational authorities in Northern Ireland have funded a program (Dunn & Morgan, 1999) designed to encourage contact between Catholic and Protestant schools and more recently have funded the development of planned integrated schools. These educational initiatives relate to structural change as well as content and curriculum development, and are loosely based on assumptions derived from social identity theory and the contact hypothesis. This article aims to inform practitioners about the most effective ways of implementing intergroup contact in education in the context of conflict, whether experienced as political violence or as community divisions such as increasing multiculturalism. Although Northern Ireland represents an example of a (post) conflict society, it nevertheless provides a useful context for the broader examination of educational initiatives aimed at promoting social cohesion and peace. The use of an appropriate theoretical framework facilitates the exploration of relevant concepts in Northern Ireland and allows conclusions to be drawn that are relevant to other contexts, including societies with different experiences of peace and conflict.

Violent Conflict in Northern Ireland

The need to promote contact between groups arises because of the long-standing conflict between the Protestants/Unionists/Loyalists, who wish to see Northern Ireland remain part of the United Kingdom and make up about 50% of the population, and the Catholics/Nationalists/Republicans, who wish to see the unification of the island of Ireland and make up about 40% of the population (Cairns & Darby, 1998). Though the conflict has lasted for centuries, today it has become a melange of historical, religious, political, economic, and psychological elements. In the last 30 years the conflict was at its most virulent, resulting in many deaths and injuries, plus psychological stress and increased community divisions. In the 1990s a series of cease-fires by paramilitary groups on both sides eventually led to a political agreement that became known locally to Catholics as the *Good Friday Agreement* and to Protestants as *The Belfast Agreement*. The *peace process*, as it has become known, faces political and military challenges particularly from dissidents in both communities. Therefore, though it could be argued that the violence has (almost) ended, the conflict goes on and the need to promote contact continues.

The Contact Hypothesis

The contact hypothesis has been the major influence underpinning cross-community programs, including educational initiatives, in Northern Ireland (Hughes & Knox, 1997). In its simplest form, the contact hypothesis (Allport, 1954; Hewstone & Brown, 1986; Pettigrew, 1986) proposes that bringing together individuals from opposing groups can reduce intergroup conflict "under optimal conditions" (Pettigrew & Tropp, 2000). Allport (1954) suggested four conditions to bring about contact that may lead to reduced intergroup conflict. First, there should be equal status among the groups who meet, or at least among the individuals drawn from the groups. Second, the situation in which intergroup contact occurs should require cooperation between groups or offer common goals. Third, social competition among the groups involved should be avoided. Last, the contact situation should be legitimized through institutional support.

Contact and Education

In Northern Ireland the segregated structure of the educational system was challenged most pertinently when parents lobbied for the establishment of integrated schools, which would draw approximately equal numbers of Catholic and Protestant pupils, with the "aim of providing for them an effective education that gives equal recognition to and promotes equal expression of the two major traditions" (Northern Ireland Council for Integrated Education, 2004). As a result, the first integrated school was established in Belfast in 1981. Over the last 20 years this movement has grown slowly but steadily (Gallagher, Smith, & Montgomery, 2003) and has led to the establishment of some 57 integrated primary and secondary schools to date. Today, though still constituting a minority of schools in Northern Ireland and only catering to about 5% of the total pupil population (Gallagher et al., 2003), integrated schools receive government funding and provide an alternative for parents wishing to break out of the straightjacket of segregated denominational-based schooling.

This major structural change was accompanied by changes to the curricular content in a variety of subject areas. The Education Reform Order (1989) introduced a national curriculum taught in all schools in Northern Ireland. This includes a common curriculum for those subjects that are often associated with community relations, such as history and religious education (Arlow, 2003). Most important, all schools are required to incorporate community relations into their teaching through the introduction of the statutory and cross-curricular themes known as Education for Mutual Understanding (EMU) and Cultural Heritage (CH; Arlow, 2003; Gallagher, 2003). EMU has been widely criticized since its introduction because of its too narrow content, which focuses on community relations between Catholics and Protestants only; its peripheral nature to the curriculum due to its cross-curricular nature; and, more practically, its lack of sufficient training to enable teachers to cope with controversial issues that might arise (Montgomery & McCully, 2000). Partly as result of these criticisms, new curriculum proposals have been made to promote the introduction of Local and Global Citizenship Education to address previous initiatives' shortcomings (Smith, 2003). In addition to the mandatory curricular changes, a separate voluntary program, known as the School Community Relations Programme, was introduced to promote cross-community contact between Catholic and Protestant pupils from segregated schools.

Research Evidence

Until recently there had been relatively little consistent research in Northern Ireland relating specifically to the proposed conditions under which contact is believed to be successful (Allport, 1954). As Cairns and Hewstone (2002) pointed out, little detail is known about the possible theoretical underpinnings of cross-community schemes in Northern Ireland, except that they involve some form of cross-community contact. Hughes and Knox (1997), for example, note that, though conditions such as superordinate goals, cooperation, and equal status are recognized as valuable in practice, they are rarely given strategic priority. The problem lies with the fact that most of the research in Northern Ireland that investigated the impact of the contact hypothesis was outcome oriented rather than process oriented. In our following review we will therefore discuss separately the earlier outcome-oriented research that is often child based (see Trew, 1986, for a review) and the more recent process-oriented research that is largely adult based (e.g., Cairns et al., 1993; Hargie et al., 1999).

Outcome Research

In general, the early research provided modest but relatively consistent evidence that cross-community contact was positively associated with reducing negative outgroup attitudes. However, questions were raised about the generalizability of such positive outcomes to a broader societal level. As a result, cross-community contact was recommended as a remedy to deteriorating intergroup relations and, sometimes, contact in itself was seen as a measure of success (Cairns & Hewstone, 2002). Often such contact involved short-term educational interventions and were more common in the 1980s. Trew (1986) concluded that, although belonging to different denominations did not preclude the development of friendships as a result of short-term contact, there was no evidence that "contact *per se* will either influence salient political beliefs or have any impact on sectarianism in the society" (p. 105). Trew also pointed out that the quality of cross-community friendships often differed from intra-community friendships in that potentially controversial issues, such as politics or religion, were avoided in conversations.

Since the introduction of the School Community Relations Programme and the development of the integrated education sector, research into the impact of these educational initiatives on pupils' attitudes and social identities has grown steadily, though no systematic longitudinal research has been conducted (Abbott et al., 1998). One of the first studies (Irwin, 1991) found an increase in the number and duration of intercommunity friendships among current pupils and those who had recently completed their education. Similarly, in a study of integrated and desegregated schools (McClenahan, Cairns, Dunn, & Morgan, 1996), it was suggested that cross-community friendships were increased by intergroup contact. A recent survey comparing pupils from integrated schools with pupils from segregated postprimary schools (Stringer et al., 2000) has gone further and indicated that integrated education positively impacts the quality and quantity of outgroup friendships and pupils' attitudes to integration. Support for these findings has come from a survey of former students at integrated schools (McGlynn, 2001) that also indicated integrated education may impact pupils' social identities by challenging interpretations of group identification.

A recent Review of the School Community Relations Programme (O'Connor, Hartop, & McCully, 2002) explored the nature of cross-community programs in which schools were involved and the extent to which these initiatives were perceived to be successful. Results derived from document analyses and interviews with key figures in education indicated that schools often introduced contact without adequate attention to optimal conditions being met, and teachers sometimes avoided discussions of controversial issues. Additionally, support from senior management and other teaching staff, as well as adequate teacher training, were considered to be crucial for the successful implementation of contact schemes, confirming the contact hypothesis and reflecting previous research.

Regarding curricular initiatives, as part of a wide-ranging review commissioned by the Department of Education to examine the impact and progress of Education for Mutual Understanding and Cultural Heritage, Smith and Robinson (1996) reported that there was limited evidence of direct educational benefits. Schools often only applied a minimalist approach to these cross-curricular subjects by focusing on topics not associated with the conflict and by avoiding controversial issues.

More recently, Kilpatrick and Leitch (2004) conducted a qualitative study to explore the impact of the troubles on the educational experiences of teachers and young people and the impact of educational initiatives aimed at reducing negative outgroup attitudes. Cross-community programs in the surveyed schools rarely went beyond polite exchange or addressed controversial issues. Adequate teacher training was again pointed out as an essential prerequisite for these initiatives to be successful. The research indicated that the long-term sustainability of projects was regarded as a key issue, as was the reduction of intergroup anxiety by strengthening ingroup identity. Intracommunity interventions, or *single identity work* as it is referred to in Northern Ireland, is the exploration of social identity and community relations within the community with the aim to strengthen collective self-esteem. Single identity work was perceived to be a useful step before initiating encounters between communities (Joined in Equity, Diversity and Interdependence [JEDI], 2002; Kilpatrick & Leitch, 2004).

Early research focused mainly on quantity of contact as an *input* variable and attitude change as an *output* variable largely in educational settings. More recent research, based either on university students or random sample surveys of the Northern Irish population, takes into account the quality of contact, including positive or negative experiences, and inclusion of discussion of controversial issues (Cairns, Gallagher, & Dunn, 1993; Hargie, Dickson, & Rainie, 1999). In addition, attitudinal change is no longer seen as the only outcome of successful contact, evident in studies exploring a range of possible outcomes such as increased empathy, forgiveness, and perspective taking. Finally, this recent research has attempted to go beyond outcome analyses and to focus on processes by investigating the circumstances that determine when contact will be successful and the mechanisms that influence how positive contact actually works.

Process Research

Hewstone, Cairns, Voci, Hamberger, and Niens (in press) undertook secondary analyses of data provided by the Northern Ireland Social Attitude

Surveys from 1989 and 1991. The objective was to develop a theoretical model of intergroup contact in the Northern Ireland context. Results were analyzed separately for Catholic and Protestant respondents and path analyses indicated that social class was the best predictor of contact for Protestants whereas education was the best predictor of contact for Catholics. In turn, outgroup contact consistently predicted outgroup attitudes whereas integrated education and outgroup contact were correlated. However, the effect of integrated education on outgroup contact was inconsistent across samples. The measurement of some of the key variables in the original surveys was limited, a problem remedied in subsequent research. Niens, Cairns, and Hewstone (2003) investigated possible antecedents of outgroup attitudes using a contact model proposing intergroup anxiety as a mediating variable for the positive impact of quality and quantity of contact on outgroup attitudes. Results of a random sample survey of the Northern Irish adult population supported the hypothesized relationships between quantity and quality of contact and intergroup anxiety and outgroup attitudes, with intergroup anxiety serving as a mediating variable (Hewstone et al., 2004; Niens, Cairns, & Hewstone, 2003).

Finally, using a retrospective approach, a cohort of undergraduate students at a university in Northern Ireland was surveyed in 1999 to investigate the relationship between quantity and quality of intergroup contact prior to third-level education on social identity and forgiveness (Niens, Cairns, Hewstone, & McLernon, 2003). As expected, the overall quantity of contact and experience with cross-community schemes impacted negatively on group identification and positively on the perceived quality of contact. Integrated education was positively associated with the perceived quality of outgroup contact, though it was not significantly associated with group identification. In turn, the quality of contact was negatively correlated with strength of group identification. Though quality of contact impacted positively on forgiveness, group identification impacted negatively on it (McGlynn, Niens, Cairns, & Hewstone, 2004).

The extended contact hypothesis (Wright, Aron, McLaughlin-Volpe, & Ropp, 1997) proposes that intergroup contact can be effective in reducing intergroup anxiety and promoting positive outgroup attitudes even when experienced only indirectly through reports of a significant other. Research conducted by Paolini, Hewstone, Cairns, and Voci (2004) explored assumptions derived from this extended contact hypothesis. Results from a student survey and a random sample survey of the Northern Ireland adult population indicated that direct and indirect contact predicted outgroup attitudes, a relationship that was mediated by reduced intergroup anxiety. This has implications for a possible ripple effect from the currently small integrated educational sector.

Conclusions

From the research evidence reported earlier and research conducted beyond Northern Ireland (e.g., Pettigrew & Tropp, 2000), the practitioner planning to implement cross-community contact schemes or working in a mixed community environment with the aim of promoting positive intergroup relations (such as integrated schools) could draw the following conclusions:

1. Intergroup contact may help to promote a positive outcome if implemented using the optimal conditions that promote altered intergroup attitudes. Generally, research supports the usefulness of Allport's (1954) conditions for the promotion of effective intergroup contact. For contact to be successful, participants of similar status should work collaboratively to achieve common goals.

2. Competitive situations should be avoided.

3. Institutional support in the form of backing from senior management and other teaching staff is also recognized as crucial in successfully implementing intergroup contact, or indeed any kind of value initiatives, in the formal education system (Osler & Starkey, 1998) or teacher training (Ross, 1999).

4. The quality of contact needs to be monitored carefully to ensure that contact with outgroup members is, overall, experienced as positive and friendships are formed. This is particu-

larly important in the light of research emphasizing the need for the contact situation to provide scope for more than a superficial exchange.

5. Intergroup anxiety and social identity appear to be key factors explaining the process through which contact impacts on outgroup attitudes. Reduction of intergroup anxiety could be regarded as one key outcome of intergroup contact and should be taken into account when introducing contact (possibly through employing prior single identity work) and when monitoring the success of contact initiatives.

6. Finally, long-term sustainability of contact appears to be a key issue and is widely acknowledged as such in the literature in Northern Ireland.

Though these factors are relatively well documented, more recent research indicates possible benefits of extended contact that is experienced second-hand through reports of ingroup members. For the practitioner, this would mean providing the opportunity for participants in an intergroup contact intervention to relate their experiences to their peers who have not been exposed to intergroup contact. Because this is the least researched benefit accruing from cross-community contact, it would be necessary to monitor and evaluate this process closely. More research is required to establish the most beneficial sequence in which cross-community contact needs to be introduced in different contexts.

Although this article addresses conflict, contact, and education within the context of Northern Ireland, the research has implications for other practitioners. Northern Ireland has, over the last 30 years, become a useful testing ground for educational practices that can contribute to the reduction of community divisions. As such, it may provide a useful example to other societies, where community divisions and segregation also represent obstacles to social inclusion and harmonious intergroup relations.

References

Abbott, L., Dunn, S., & Morgan, V. (1998) *Integrated Education in Northern Ireland: An Analytical Review*. Coleraine, Northern Ireland: Centre for the Study of Conflict, University of Ulster.

Allport, G. W. (1954). *The nature of prejudice*. Reading, MA: Addison-Wesley.

Arlow, M. (2003). *Northern Ireland: Synopsis of the case study*. Retrieved October 10, 2004, from http://www.ibe.unesco.org/Regional/social_cohesion/pdf/synni.pdf

Cairns, E. (1987). *Caught in crossfire: Children in Northern Ireland*. Belfast, Northern Ireland: Appletree; Syracuse, NY: Syracuse University Press.

Cairns, E., & Darby, J. (1998). The conflict in Northern Ireland: Causes, consequences, and controls. *American Psychologist, 53*, 754–760.

Cairns, E., Gallagher, A. M., & Dunn, S. (1993). *Intergroup contact in a Northern Irish university setting: A report to the Central Community Relations Unit*. Coleraine, Northern Ireland: Centre for the Study of Conflict, University of Ulster.

Cairns, E., & Hewstone, M. (2002). The impact of peacemaking in Northern Ireland on intergroup behaviour. In G. Salomon & B. Nevo (Eds.), *The nature and study of peace education* (pp. 217–228). Mahwah, NJ: Lawrence Erlbaum Associates, Inc.

Darby, J., Murray, D., Batts, D., Dunn, S., Farren, S., & Harris, J. (1977). *Education and community in Northern Ireland: Schools apart?* Coleraine, Northern Ireland: Centre for the Study of Conflict, University of Ulster.

Dunn, S., & Morgan, V. (1999). A fraught path–Education as a basis for developing community relations in Northern Ireland. *Oxford Review of Education, 25*, 141–153.

Education Reform (Northern Ireland) Order. (1989). *S.I 1989, No. 2406 (NI20)*. Belfast, Northern Ireland: Her Majesty's Stationery Office.

Gallagher, A. M. (1995). The approach of government: Community relations and equity. In S. Dunn (Ed.), *Facets of the conflict in Northern Ireland* (pp. 27–43). New York: St. Martin's Press.

Gallagher, T. (2003). Education and equality in Northern Ireland. In O. Hargie & D. Dickson (Eds.), *Researching the Troubles: Social science perspectives on the Northern Ireland conflict* (pp. 59–83). Edinburgh, Scotland: Mainstream.

Gallagher, T., Smith, A., & Montgomery, A. (2003). *Integrated education in Northern Ireland: Participation, profile and performance*. Coleraine, Northern Ireland: UNESCO Centre, University of Ulster.

Hargie, O. D. W., Dickson, D. A., & Rainie, S. (1999). *Communication and relational development among young adult Catholics and Protestants: A report to* the Central Community Relations Unit. Jordanstown, Northern Ireland: University of Ulster.

Hewstone, M., & Brown, R. (1986). Contact is not enough: An intergroup perspective on the contact hypothesis. In M. Hewstone & R. Brown (Eds.), *Contact and conflict in intergroup encounters* (pp. 3–44). Oxford, UK: Basil Blackwell.

Hewstone, M., Cairns, E., Voci, A., Hamberger, J., & Niens, U. (in press). Intergroup contact, forgiveness, and experience of 'The Troubles' in Northern Ireland. *Journal of Social Issues*.

Hewstone, M., Cairns, E., Voci, A., McLernon, F., Niens, U., & Noor, M. (2004). Intergroup forgiveness and guilt in Northern Ireland: Social psychological dimensions of 'The Troubles.' In N. R. Branscombe & B. Doosje (Eds.), *Collective guilt: International perspectives* (pp. 193–215). New York: Cambridge University Press.

Hughes, J., & Knox, C. (1997). *Ten years wasted effort?—An overview of community relations in Northern Ireland: A report to the Central Community Relations Unit*. Jordanstown, Northern Ireland: University of Ulster.

Irwin, C. (1991). *Education and the development of social integration in divided societies*. Belfast, Northern Ireland: Queens University of Belfast.

Joined in Equity, Diversity and Interdependence. (JEDI). (2002). *Community relations and education for citizenship with the Northern Ireland youth service*. Belfast, Northern Ireland: Author.

Kilpatrick, R., & Leitch, R. (2004). Teachers' and pupils' educational experiences and school-based responses to the conflict in Northern Ireland. *Journal of Social Issues, 54*, 563–586.

Knox, C., & Hughes, J. (1996). Crossing the divide: Community relations in Northern Ireland. *Journal of Peace Research, 33*, 83–98.

McClenahan, C., Cairns, E., Dunn, S., & Morgan, V. (1996). Intergroup friendships: Integrated and desegregated schools in Northern Ireland. *The Journal of Social Psychology, 136*, 549–558.

McGlynn, C. W. (2001). *The impact of post primary integrated education in Northern Ireland on past pupils: A study*. Unpublished EdD thesis, University of Ulster, Coleraine, Northern Ireland.

McGlynn, C., Niens, U., Cairns, E., & Hewstone, M. (2004). Moving out of conflict: The contribution of integrated schools in Northern Ireland to identity, attitudes, forgiveness and reconciliation. *Journal of Peace Education, 1*, 147–163.

Montgomery, A., & McCully, A. (2000). What have values got to do with it? In G. Easdown (Ed.), *Innovation and methodology: Opportunities and constraints in history teacher education* (pp. 55–66). Lancaster: St. Martin's College.

Niens, U., Cairns, E., & Hewstone, M. (2003). Contact and conflict in Northern Ireland. In O. Hargie & D. Dickson (Eds.), *Researching the Troubles: Social science perspectives on the Northern Ireland conflict* (pp. 123–140). Edinburgh, Scotland: Mainstream.

Niens, U., Cairns, E., Hewstone, M., & McLernon, F. (2003, September). *Intergroup contact in education: Impact on forgiveness*. Paper presented at the Conference for Peacebuilding After Peace Accords. Joan B. Kroc Institute for International Peace Studies, University of Notre Dame, South Bend, IN.

Northern Ireland Council for Integrated Education. (2004). Aims and objectives. Retrieved November 11, 2002, from http://www.nicie.org/aboutus/default.asp?id=25

O'Connor, U., Hartop, B., & McCully, A. (2002). *A review of the School Community Relations Programme 2002*. Retrieved November 19, 2004, from http://www.deni.gov.uk/about/consultation/documents/Review_of_Schools_CR_Prog.pdf

Osler, A., & Starkey, H. (1998). Children's rights and citizenship: Some implications for the management of schools. *The International Journal of Children's Rights, 6*, 313–333.

Paolini, S., Hewstone, M., Cairns, E., & Voci, A. (2004). Effects of direct and indirect cross-group friendships on judgments of Catholics and Protestants in Northern Ireland: The mediating role of an anxiety-reduction mechanism. *Personality and Social Psychology Bulletin, 30*, 770–786.

Pettigrew, T. F. (1986). The intergroup contact hypothesis reconsidered. In M. Hewstone & R. Brown (Eds.), *Contact and conflict in intergroup encounters* (pp. 169–195). Oxford, UK: Basil Blackwell.

Pettigrew, T. F., & Tropp, L. R. (2000). Does intergroup contact reduce prejudice?: Recent meta-analytic findings. In S. Oskamp (Ed.), *Reducing prejudice and discrimination. "The Claremont Symposium on Applied Social Psychology"* (pp. 93–114). Mahwah, NJ: Lawrence Erlbaum Associates, Inc.

Ross, A. (1999). Some reflections on citizenship in the national curriculum. *Primary Teaching Studies, 11*, 20–23.

Smith, A. (2003). Citizenship education in Northern Ireland: Beyond national identity? *Cambridge Journal of Education, 33*, 15–31.

Smith, A., & Robinson, A. (1996). *Education for mutual understanding: The initial statutory years*.

Coleraine, Northern Ireland: Centre for the Study of Conflict, University of Ulster.

Stringer, M., Wilson, W., Irwing, P., Giles, M., McClenahan, C., & Curtis, L. (2000). *The impact of schooling on the social attitudes of children.* Belfast, Northern Ireland: The Integrated Education Fund.

Trew, K. (1986). Catholic–Protestant contact in Northern Ireland. In M. Hewstone & R. Brown (Eds.), *Contact and conflict in intergroup encounters* (pp. 93–106). Oxford, UK: Basil Blackstaff.

Wright, S. C., Aron, A., McLaughlin-Volpe, T., & Ropp, S. A. (1997). The extended contact effect: Knowledge of cross-group friendships and prejudice. *Journal of Personality and Social Psychology, 73,* 73–90.

Tricia S. Jones

Implementing Community Peace and Safety Networks in South Africa

Peace education initiatives often import American models and techniques without careful consideration of their fit with existing sociohistorical contexts, indigenous cultures, and necessary links to community. This article describes a 2-year project that instituted school- and community-based mediation programs as Community Peace and Safety Networks in the Gauteng region of South Africa. Qualitative research processes were used to conduct needs assessments and develop cultural sensitivity that increased the success of the project. The potential role of formative and summative evaluation research to enhance respect for context, culture and community are discussed in relation to peace education efforts.

Tricia S. Jones is a Professor in the Department of Psychological Studies in Education at Temple University.
  Correspondence should be addressed to Tricia S. Jones, Department of Psychological Studies in Education, Temple University, Philadelphia, PA 19122. E-mail: tsjones@temple.edu

THE PEACE EDUCATION WORKING GROUP at UNICEF defines peace education as the following:

> the process of promoting the knowledge, skills, attitudes and values needed to bring about behavior changes that will enable children, youth and adults to prevent conflict and violence, both overt and structural; to resolve conflict peacefully; and to create the conditions conducive to peace, whether at an intrapersonal, interpersonal, inter-group, national or international level. (UNESCO, 2002)

Peace education and conflict resolution education share goals and objectives (Bodine & Crawford, 1998; Jones & Compton, 2003; Sommers, 2003). Peace education programs help people develop communication skills of active listening and assertive speech, problem-solving skills of brainstorming or consensus building, and orientation skills of cultural awareness and empathy. Peace education emphasizes understanding the dynamics of social conflict, warfare, conflict resolution, and peace.

As Salomon and Nevo (2002) suggested, no typical peace education curriculum exists, though peace education programs usually include "antiracism, conflict resolution, multiculturalism, cross-cultural training and the cultivation of a generally peaceful outlook" (Salomon, 2002, p. 7). A strong emphasis is learning methods of handling conflict, such as negotiation, mediation, or facilitation. Peer mediation is a component of many peace education programs and the most common form of conflict education in the United States (Jones, 2003; Jones & Kmitta, 2000).

The challenges of peace education include the breadth of the programming, the locus of the work, and the range of the goals. As Ben porath (2003, p. 525) summarized,

> The field entitled "peace education" is in fact so broad that authors disagree on the description of the problem they wish to address and correspondingly on the proper solution, as well as on the site in which peace education is to take place.

The peace education audience typically focuses on primary and secondary school-aged children (Reardon, 2001), though some work is done in higher education, and may even extend to adult learning. Some peace educators have bold aspirations for peace education (transforming entire societies and creating cultures of peace), whereas others working in areas of recent or ongoing conflict have more modest goals (ending and preventing the current interpersonal or intergroup violence). Research on the effectiveness of peace education is almost exclusively focused on programs that develop individual skill and alter individual attitudes rather than demonstrating impacts at group, social, or institutional levels (Ardizzone, 2003; Harris, 2003; Salomon & Nevo, 2002).

Due to the underlying mission of peace education, organizations like the Association for Childhood Education (Bayer & Staley, 2002–2003) support efforts such as the Global Campaign for Peace Education (Reardon, 2002) and the Hague Appeal for Peace (Harris & Synott, 2002). To continue growing the support for peace education, it is imperative that peace educators work to address criticisms that can be leveled at these efforts.

Peace education may be ineffective or counterproductive if it fails to respect the socio-historical–political contexts in which it is being introduced, denies the critical role of the surrounding communities, or is insensitive to the cultural realities of the people involved. This article presents a brief recounting of a peace education initiative, funded by the United States Information Agency, that created Community Peace and Safety Networks (CPSN) in South Africa following the end of apartheid. These reflections are meant to highlight the need to respect context, community, and culture, and they describe some of the ways we attempted to do this in the CPSN project. Of course, this project is not intended to serve as a model of ideal implementation, but rather as an exemplar from which to raise important issues for peace educators.

An Overview of the CPSN Project

A CPSN was created in the Gauteng province of South Africa during 1995–1997. It consisted of peer-mediation programs developed in four high schools in the Johannesburg region: an exclusively Black high school in the Black township of Thokoza; an exclusively Black high school in the Black township of Soweto; a recently integrated, predominantly Afrikaans high school; and a recently integrated girls' Catholic school in a British suburb. These school-based mediation programs were linked to four small community mediation centers established in the communities surrounding the schools.

CPSN extends the impact of school-based mediation programs by involving the school, a community conflict management organization, and community members (for example police, clergy, business owners, or representatives of other community groups; Jones & Bodtker, 1999b). Evaluation of peer-mediation program effectiveness in Philadelphia (Jones & Carlin, 1994) indicated that the positive effects of peer-mediation programs may be mitigated by a surrounding neighborhood or community that fails to understand or support the new skills and orientations taught in the schools. Without a base of education in the community, the peer-mediation efforts are limited in their effect. Involving school and community enhances the prospects for synergy and lasting effect (Jones & Bodtker, 1999a).

The project activities consisted of several phases. The phases are briefly described here and some are elaborated on in later discussions of attention to context, culture, and community. In Phase 1, a planning phase, a team of South African educators and conflict specialists (members representing each of the high schools and a South African nongovernmental organization) was brought to the United States to meet with educators and conflict specialists. Phase 2 emphasized needs assessment and community immersion with members of the U.S. team going to the South African schools and communities. In Phase 3, community-mediation trainings were delivered in South Africa. During Phase 4 the school-based mediation programs were implemented. Phase 5 involved program assessments and planning for sustainability after the funding period.

As a multicultural, multinational, longitudinal peace education effort, the CPSN project was guided by several sensibilities described by Ferdig (2001) as critical to any conflict transformation. The first is the *spirit of freedom*, in which everyone is empowered to make decisions about what to look at, how to understand events, and how to interact with others. The second sensibility is the *spirit of inclusion*—acknowledging and valuing difference. The third sensibility is the *spirit of inquiry*—looking for possibilities and options previously unconsidered.

Respecting Context

In any peace education program it is imperative that the social, historical, and political context be appreciated and allowed to influence the design and implementation of the effort. Failure to attend seriously to context results in ill-conceived *parachute* processes in which peace educators come in with short-term strategies that are rarely successful and may be destructive (Tidwell, 2004; Yarn, 2002). In the CPSN project, respecting context meant appreciating the historical magnitude of the shift from apartheid, embracing a spirit of reconciliation nationally in South Africa, and acknowledging the role the South African educational system played in this national transformation.

The significance of the spirit of reconciliation in South Africa, especially in the mid 1990s, cannot be overstated (Sparks, 2004) and was a determining factor in the decision to use a peace education initiative that was congruent with a reconciliatory frame. The Truth and Reconciliation Commission was a backdrop emphasizing general principles of peace education (Enslin, 2002; Gibson, 2004). It underscored the possibility of having offenders and victims face their previous acts and progress toward peaceful coexistence.

Critics of mediation programs in the United States had argued that, because mediation discourages blame and the attribution of responsibility for an injustice, it cannot be used as a vehicle to right the wrongs of an oppressive system (Bettman & Moore, 1994; Townley, 1994). But it was precisely the eschewing of blame that allowed mediation to embody the essence of a reconciliatory system, one of the reasons that initial peace education efforts (including mediation) in South Africa had begun in some schools (Akanda, 1995; MacDonald, 1990; Stead, 1996).

As mentioned earlier, one challenge for peace educators is the decision about locus of activity—particularly whether the initiatives should be school based. A respect for context led us to decide that school-based programs were a critical component of the peace education work we were undertaking.

There were three reasons for the emphasis on school-based conflict programs as a means of effecting social change. First, the damage that had been done in the apartheid era struck most at the youth of the country (Fourie, 1990), and interventions needed to be youth oriented. Children, especially in the townships, had been subjected to continuous violence before and after apartheid (Gibson, 1989; Swartz & Levett, 1989). Straker, Mendelsohn, and Tudin (1996) studied the perceptions of violence among South African youth in the apartheid and postapartheid periods and found that Black-on-Black violence changed from politically motivated violence to domestic and random violence following the repeal of apartheid. Peace education could reverse these conditions. As Dovey (1994, p. 9) stated, "(the youth) are … often insufficiently equipped to channel their idealism constructively. They need to have opportunities to understand, question, and challenge how society operates and how they can influence peaceful change in a positive way."

Second, schools were a primary means of enculturation (Tidwell, 2004). After apartheid, educational institutions were seen as the primary agent of social reform. Since 1994, government policy in South Africa had strongly emphasized education for peace and democracy. According to the Department of Education White Paper on Education and Training (Department of Education, 1995),

> The education system must counter the legacy of violence by promoting the values underlying democratic processes and the charter of fundamental rights, the importance of due process of law and exercise of civic responsibility and by teaching the values and skills for conflict management and conflict resolution, the importance of mediation and the benefits of tolerance and cooperation. (Harver, 2003, p. 82)

Third, given the changes in educational policy in postapartheid South Africa, schools were becoming more quickly integrated than other institutions. Tihanyi and du Toit (in press) noted that youth, especially in multiracial schools, were at the forefront of the postapartheid transformation. They were probably the first in their family to attend institutions where different race groups shared educational facilities and experienced interracial contact with the opportunity for firsthand exploration of reconciliation.

Still, with all of these reasons for engaging in school-based peace education, the question of quality in South African schools was an important aspect of context in terms of goals and implementation specifics. The schools involved were radically unequal in terms of resources, because the apartheid government had instituted highly unequal educational opportunities and facilities divided on the basis of race. The Thokoza and Soweto schools did not have windows, books, or heating, whereas the Afrikaans and British schools were as well resourced as typical suburban U.S. high schools. Fiske and Ladd (2004), in their excellent account of the changes in South African education since apartheid, recounted that in a mere decade the new regime has created an educational policy that comes close to treating races equally. The persistence of socioeconomic disparities among schools, however, means there are still substantial inequalities in educational experience and opportunity.

The schools themselves were undergoing considerable structural changes. The end of apartheid ushered in a number of significant educational reforms, such as the centralization of a previously (racially) divided education administration, the introduction of new curricula, and the racial integration of schools (Tihanyi & du Toit, in press). One of the biggest changes was the policy reallocating teachers to schools they would previously not have entered. For example, it was common for a teacher of a well-resourced school in his or her community to be assigned to an impoverished township or border area school. As a result, many teachers quit and many new teachers were hired without adequate training. Two studies conducted during this time (Rogan, 1999; Taylor & Vinjevold, 1999) found that, in most schools, lack of teacher education resulted in overreliance on lecture formats, inability to teach in students' native languages, poorly structured lessons and curricula, little group or participatory work among students, and even little emphasis on reading and writing. Some suggest that, although progress has been made, these basic problems continue to this day (Fiske & Ladd, 2004; Onwu & Mogari, 2004; Waghid, 2004).

The context of the CPSN peace education project indicated there were realities that must be addressed in the design and implementation of the program. Clearly, a youth-based focus was needed, and schools in South Africa were the best mechanism for education. But it was not wise to rely solely on the school, or to place too much responsibility for success on undertrained teachers and school administrators undergoing stressful change and possibly planning to leave the teaching profession.

Due to these realities, we made several changes in the CPSN design. In the original project planning, we had assumed that teachers would be trained as site leadership teams for each school and run the peer-mediation programs (as in many U.S. peer-mediation programs), that the school-based programs would be implemented first and the community programs created second, and that the concentration would be on a community-by-community design rather than a network crossing all communities. All of these plans were modified based on the factors previously discussed. Although teachers were trained in mediation with students, the focus shifted to a much greater student-empowerment model, and the training shifted to accommodate that. The initial phases of training asked students to discuss the purposes of mediation and peace education in their schools and communities. The students identified the goals and structures for the programs that were included into program design. The community-based programs were developed first, and their implementation highlighted the need for strong community support. Perhaps most important, the decision was made to build infrastructures between schools and communities in the project as much as possible. For example, trainings were structured to combine students from various schools to increase their experience of meeting and working with new and different peers.

Respecting Community

Arguing that community support can be important to educational innovation is not new. Knoff's (1995) model of improving school-community relations emphasizes that there must be human resource systems in the school that are linked to the wider community, that truly partner with the community in a collaborative fashion, and where teacher involvement in these collaborations is key. One of the reasons these links to community are key, according to Knoff, is that they help innovators develop an understanding of deep cultures and help participants generate shared norms and cultures. Yet even with the advocacy for community linkage, the reality is often disappointing. Most educational interventions do not build successful partnerships with the surrounding community.

Other peace education experiences have also confirmed that community involvement can determine the success of peace education. Looking at peace and reconciliation work in Northern Ireland, Cairns (1996) and Smith (2002) confirmed that school-based initiatives require community links and support to succeed. Although school-based programs may be able to develop individual skills, without involvement of students in the community and involvement of community members in the program, the skills wane and the impacts to intergroup and social peace building do not happen (Williams, 2004).

The decision to develop Community Peace and Safety Networks signaled an initial respect for community gained from the grassroots peace education work that some of the project principals had conducted in the United States (Jones & Bodtker, 1999a). Yet, in addition to including the community, we took several actions to respect the community as a partner in the peace education efforts.

First, we wanted to build in time to meet and learn from the four South African communities as well as the schools. This was done in several ways. As a condition for receiving funding we had completed initial orientation with South African community members, but in the Phase 1 planning we realized that this was not nearly sufficient. As a result we added Phase 2, devoted to building relationships with community partners, in which members of the U.S. team went to South Africa and spent 2 weeks meeting with community members and school members. Specifically, Phase 2 provided us with an opportunity to make presentations at the schools, meet with community leaders, and gather information about their needs, desires, and resources through focus group interviews and informal discussions. The emphasis on qualitative and quantitative needs assessment as essential for planning and design was perhaps the most important factor in the overall CPSN project accomplishments.

Second, we started the mediation training in the communities so we could have some support for the mediation when we introduced it in the schools. The community support was not difficult to gain in the Black townships where tribal cultures have long resonated with the use of informal third party processes like mediation for resolving disputes (Gibson, 2004). In fact, the number of adults ultimately trained as mediators for the community mediation centers in Thokoza and Soweto were double the initial projections. But the Afrikaans and British communities were not as sanguine about developing community-mediation centers. They were satisfied with having adults trained in mediation to act as support for the schools, but were reluctant to go the next step.

Throughout Phases 3 and 4 we made as much time as possible (outside of training) to visit communities, spend time with school and community members, and continue the dialogue of how the project was meeting their needs. And, of course, between phases the members of the South African project team were working in their communities spreading the word and building support. They did an excellent job of identifying community leaders and stakeholders whose support would be key for maintaining the project focus after funding. Policymakers at the municipal level, from the private sectors, the Department of Education, and the Department of Safety and Security were brought into the discussions relatively early in the project. This involvement helped to move toward institutionalization of the conflict education initiatives. The community support was advanced enough at the end of the project to host a 1-day conference where hundreds of community members and members of the educational infrastructure of the Gauteng province came together to celebrate the accomplishments of the Community Peace and Safety Networks (Jones, 2004).

Respecting Culture

If peace educators respect context and community it is likely that they will also be at least partially respectful of culture, given the integral relationship between these components. However, there are many levels of culture, and some of the more subtle may be underemphasized by peace educators. In their account of peace education efforts in the West African country of Sierra Leone, Bretherton, Weston, and Zbar remind us of issues of transferability and cultural insensitivity:

> The question of how valid it is to transfer the peace education curriculum from one context or culture to another is also a key issue. ... Our aim was to develop a program that suited local conditions but that also modeled what has been learned from international experience. The method adopted—drawing upon and then systematizing the work of local agencies and educators for peace—was cooperative rather than an imposition by experts. ... The need to connect with the local culture. This sounds like a truism, but is not often observed in practice. (2003, pp. 15–16)

One way we tried to respect more subtle elements of culture included analyses of the conflict-management norms of the various student cultures through a series of focus-group interviews. Before developing and implementing the peer-mediation training, it was important to understand the students' conflict contexts. This initial examination would provide critical information about whether the conflict contexts in which peer mediation was used in the United States were sufficiently similar to conflict contexts in South Africa to justify cross-cultural transferability of the training models. In addition, it would provide information about the cross-cultural differences in conflict contexts among the diverse South African student groups. Focus group interviews were analyzed for themes related to the following three areas: (a) What types of conflicts do students experience? (b) How is conflict managed by students? and (c) What opportunities for change can be identified in the way conflict is handled?

By and large, the types of conflicts reported by the South African students resembled those reported by students in U.S. schools (e.g., rumors, he said/she said, boyfriend/girlfriend disputes, disobeying rules, and arguments with teachers). Racial conflict was also reported, primarily by students in the predominately White schools, but was not posed as intractable nor did students reference vivid stereotypes. Rather, racial conflict was identified in relation to language use or preferences in music and fashion. These findings have recently been supported by other qualitative research on racial integration processes in South African high schools (Tihanyi & du Toit, in press).

Language was seen as an important cultural cue tied to conflict (e.g., which language gets privileged in interaction) and was also a source of misunderstanding between students. It is important to note that only the British students spoke English as a first language; for all other students English was a second language (or third or fourth, as is the case of most of the Black students). Yet, for the students in the CPSN project, English is the language common between them, thus their only means of interacting. Also, racial conflict related to language use was not unique to White and Black groups; the White British and Afrikaans students also used language as an intergroup marker.

Though most reported conflicts were similar among the different school groups, some differences were reported. Students in the Black schools discussed more conflicts related to family and with teachers and expressed the desire to learn how to manage these conflicts. For instance, one student wanted to know how to help his parents settle a dispute, showing great concern to bring harmony to the family. Of course, conflicts related to family and teachers were not relevant only in the Black schools. What is noteworthy, however, is that Black students chose to discuss these types of conflicts to a far greater extent than did the students from the primarily White schools. This may represent a cultural difference so that the Black student cultures place a greater emphasis on community (e.g., a collectivist culture), whereas the White student cultures are more individualistically oriented (Dovey, 1994).

Just as the types of conflicts that were reported by South African students were quite similar, so too were their modes for identifying and manifesting conflict. Most conflict was identified as disagreements or arguments, viewed as negative, and frequently framed as group or clique related. The British students spoke more of following rules and being respectful of the age and *position* hierarchy when they identified conflict, suggesting a strong normative orientation to their understanding of conflict. Conflict was manifested by exchanging verbal putdowns, chastising, spreading rumors, and nonverbally shunning or excommunicating students in disfavor.

The greatest diversity between the different student groups was in how they managed conflicts. The British students relied overwhelmingly on authority to manage their conflicts. Although they had an official structure designed to empower them to deal with conflict on their own, it was based on hierarchy according to grade and was reportedly largely unsuccessful in resolving conflict. Students also reported the use of direct confrontation, yet ensuing talk typically involved attempts to persuade one another rather than engage in genuine discussion. Thus the conflict was often left unresolved unless brought to the attention of a teacher or administrator.

On the other hand, the Afrikaans students dealt with conflict almost exclusively through peer groups and rarely consulted adults in the school to assist them. Interpersonal conflict, or conflict between members of a peer group, became a group issue, often with the leader of the group and other group members taking the responsibility of negotiating for the members in conflict. The Afrikaans students also placed a high value on face saving in this context. For instance, one boy reported that, when two boys in the peer group had an issue, the one deemed at fault was not made to explicitly admit fault; rather, it was implicitly understood through informal talk among other members of the group, and the boys went about their business as usual. If the issue had not been adequately addressed (i.e., if the injured party did not feel redeemed), they waited until another explicit issue (related or not) arose, or they created another issue, and then went through the same process. The girls at the Afrikaans school also reported that conflicts were frequently managed through silence. For example, if a girl learned that her friend had spread a rumor about her, she would actively avoid and ignore the friend rather than confront her or have others confront her.

Interestingly, the Afrikaans boys commented that, although they managed conflict among their

(White) peer groups indirectly, they believed that racial conflict in the school needed to be addressed explicitly because "there is not yet established a common understanding of *what* means *what!*" The boys went on to explain that, because the school had only been integrated for a year, the racial groups did not know each other well yet, and the process of true integration was occurring slowly.

Informed by the insights from the focus group interviews, we changed the initial plans for peer-mediation training in three ways. First we realized that combined trainings would provide some opportunities for students to work outside their own school communities. However, there were language difficulties that prohibited students from all four schools being trained together. We combined the Thokoza and Soweto schools for one training and combined the Afrikaans and British schools for a second training. It is important to note that the Afrikaans and British schools, which have been recently integrated, chose a racially and gender-diverse group of students to participate in mediation training. In Phase 4 the project provided two 4-day peer-mediation trainings for 83 secondary school students.

The second change was to make the training more multilingual. South African and U.S. trainers worked together as training teams to allow the South African trainers to present all information in English, Zulu, and Afrikaans. Written training materials and questionnaires were translated into Zulu and Afrikaans so all students could learn from materials in their first language. Although this required more coordination between trainers, the result was significant, especially among the Thokozan and Sowetan youth who found the use of their native languages a signal of respect and empowerment.

The third change was to incorporate the conflict norms for various student cultures into the training in terms of role plays, exercises, examples, and discussions. In addition, the mediation training began with a series of discussions in which students articulated how they saw mediation benefiting their schools and communities. Instead of assuming that mediation would serve the same purposes for all schools, we allowed the students to explore the possibilities and tailor the mediation process and program to reflect their cultural orientations.

Conclusion

The success of peace education in the CPSN project was significantly impacted by the context, community, and cultures involved in the project. This article provides a brief account of why those factors are important and how we tried to respect them. Peace educators should attend to these factors, especially if they are involved in school-based interventions.

Peace educators are well-served to maintain macro- and microfocuses when planning and engaging in their work. We need to resist the tendency to assume the cultural transferability of programs, curricula, and techniques. In addition, we need to resist the temptation to concentrate exclusively on the individual or the interpersonal when monitoring the impacts of peace education interventions. Changing a student's attitudes and improving a student's skills are very important, but retaining that narrow focus misses a great deal that may explain those changes as well as suggest additional impacts at group and social levels.

The considerations of context, community, and culture all require sophistication in and dedication to the use of program evaluation research. In the CPSN project we relied heavily on observation, participant observation, focus group interviews, and informal discussions at all phases of the project. Grounding in basic formative program evaluation processes helps ensure effective and respectful peace education.

References

Akanda, A. (1995). Communication—Its effect on the self-concept of children: A South African perspective. *Early Childhood Development and Care, 105,* 69–76.

Ardizzone, L. (2003). Generating peace: A study of nonformal youth organizations. *Peace & Change, 28,* 420–446.

Bayer, E., & Staley, L. (2002–2003). Teaching peace in a violent world. *Childhood Education, 79*(2), 96–97.

Ben porath S. R. (2003). War and peace education. *Journal of Philosophy of Education, 37*, 525–534.

Bettman, E. H., & Moore, P. (1994). Conflict resolution programs and social justice. *Education and Urban Society, 27*(1), 11–21.

Bodine, R., & Crawford, D. (1998). *The handbook of conflict resolution education: A guide to building quality programs in schools.* San Francisco: Jossey-Bass.

Bretherton, D., Weston, J., & Zbar, V. (2003). Peace education in a post-conflict environment: The case of Sierra Leone. *Ethos, 11*(2), 12–20.

Cairns, E. (1996). *Children and political violence.* Oxford, UK: Blackwell.

Department of Education. (1995). *White paper on education and training.* Pretoria, South Africa: Author.

Dovey, V. (1994). *Exploring peace education in South African settings.* (ERIC Document Reproduction Service No. ED 384 542).

Enslin, P. (2002). South Africa: The Truth and Reconciliation Commission as a model of peace education. In G. Salomon & B. Nevo (Eds.), *Peace education: The concepts, principles, and practices around the world* (pp. 237–243). Mahwah, NJ: Lawrence Erlbaum Associates, Inc.

Ferdig, M. (2001). *Exploring the social construction of complex self-organizing change: A study of emerging change in the regulation of nuclear power.* Unpublished doctoral dissertation, Organizational Development, Benedictine University, Lisle, IL.

Fiske, E. B., & Ladd, H. F. (2004). *Elusive equity: Education reform in post-apartheid South Africa.* Washington, DC: Brookings.

Fourie, E. (1990). The UN convention on the rights of the child and the crisis for children in South Africa: Apartheid and detention. *Human Rights Quarterly, 12*, 106–114.

Gibson, J. L. (2004). *Overcoming apartheid: Can truth reconcile a divided nation?* New York: Sage.

Gibson, K. (1989). Children in political violence. *Social Science and Medicine, 28*, 659–667.

Harris, I. M. (2003). Peace education at the end of a bloody century. *Educational Studies, 34*, 336–351.

Harris, I., & Synott, J. (2002). Guest editors' introduction: Peace education for a new century. *Social Alternatives, 21*(1), 3–7.

Harver, C. (2003). Safe schools: Violence and the struggle for peace and democracy in South African education. In E. Uwazie (Ed.), *Conflict resolution and peace education in Africa* (pp. 77–87). Oxford, UK: Lexington.

Jones, T. S. (2003). Proven benefits of conflict resolution education. In P. von Tongeren (Ed.), *Proceedings of the International Conference on Conflict Resolution Education* (pp. 57–68). Soesterberg, The Netherlands: European Center for Conflict Prevention.

Jones, T. S. (2004). Enhancing collaborative tendencies: Extending the single identity model for youth conflict education. *New Directions in Youth Development, 102*, 11–34.

Jones, T. S., & Bodtker, A. (1999a). *Final report: Community peace and safety networks.* Philadelphia: Pennsylvania Commission on Crime and Delinquency, Governor's Special Project Fund.

Jones, T. S., & Bodtker, A. (1999b). Guidelines for successful peer mediation programs. In D. Schnitman & S. Littlejohn (Eds.), *Mediation: Perspectives, practices and domains* (pp. 143–156). Buenos Aires, Argentina: Paidos.

Jones, T. S., & Carlin, D. (1994). *Preliminary report of the Philadelphia Peer Mediation Project: 1992–1994.* Unpublished report, Temple University, Philadelphia.

Jones, T. S., & Compton, R. O. (Eds.). (2003). *Kids working it out: Stories and strategies for making peace in our nation's schools.* San Francisco: Jossey-Bass.

Jones, T. S., & Kmitta, D. (Eds.). (2000). *Does it work? The case for conflict resolution education in our nation's schools.* Washington, DC: Conflict Resolution Education Network.

Knoff, H. N. (1995). Best practice in facilitating school-based organizational change and strategic planning. In A. Thomas & J. Grimes (Eds.), *Best practices in school psychology III* (pp. 112–132). Bethesda, MD: National Association of School Psychologists.

MacDonald, C. A. (1990). *Crossing the threshold into standard three in Black education: The consolidated main report of the Threshold project.* Pretoria, South Africa: Human Sciences Research Council. (ERIC Document Reproduction Service No. ED 344 469)

Onwu, G., & Mogari, D. (2004). Professional development for outcomes-based education curriculum implementation: the case of UNIVEMALASHI, South Africa. *Journal of Education for Teaching, 30*, 161–178.

Reardon, B. A. (2001). *Education for a culture of peace in a gender perspective.* Paris: UNESCO.

Reardon, B. A. (2002). Human rights and the global campaign for peace education. *International Review of Education, 48*(3/4), 283–285.

Rogan, J. (1999). The implementation of Curriculum 2005: A research agenda. In E. Fennema & K. Taole (Eds.), *Proceedings of the second joint conference: Mapping out a research agenda to drive professional development in systemic reform* (pp. 44–57). Pretoria, South Africa: NSF, USA, NRF.

Salomon, G. (2002). The nature of peace education: Not all programs are created equal. In G. Salomon & B. Nevo (Eds.), *Peace education: The concept, principles and practices around the world* (pp. 3–36). London: Lawrence Erlbaum Associates, UK.

Salomon, G., & Nevo, B. (Eds.). (2002). *Peace education: The concepts, principles, and practices around the world.* Mahwah, NJ: Lawrence Erlbaum Associates, Inc.

Smith, R. (2002). Professional educational psychology and community relations: Education in Northern Ireland. *Educational Psychology in Practice, 18,* 275–296.

Sommers, M. (2003, August 11–15). *Peace education: Opportunities and challenges.* Paper presented at the Building Bridges to Peace and Prosperity: Education and Training for Action, US Agency for International Development, Washington, DC.

Sparks, A. (2004). *Beyond the miracle: Inside the new South Africa.* Chicago: University of Chicago Press.

Stead, G. B. (1996). Career development of Black South African adolescents: A developmental–contextual perspective. *Journal of Counseling and Development, 74,* 270–275.

Straker, G., Mendelsohn, F. M., & Tudin, P. (1996). Violent political contexts and the emotional concerns of township youth. *Child Development, 67,* 46–54.

Swartz, L., & Levett, A. (1989). Political repression and children in South Africa: The social construction of damaging effects. *Social Science and Medicine, 28,* 741–750.

Taylor, N., & Vinjevold, P. (Eds.). (1999). *Getting learning right: Report of the President's Education Initiative Research Project.* Pretoria, South Africa: Joint Educational Trust.

Tidwell, A. (2004). Conflict, peace and education: A tangled web. *Conflict Resolution Quarterly, 21,* 463–470.

Tihanyi, K. Z., & du Toit, F. (in press). Reconciliation through integration? An examination of South Africa's reconciliation process in racially integrating high schools. *Conflict Resolution Quarterly.*

Townley, A. (1994). Conflict resolution, diversity, and social justice. *Education and Urban Society, 27*(1), 5–10.

UNESCO. (2002). *International Bureau of Education thesaurus* (6th ed.). Geneva, Switzerland: UNESCO.

Waghid, Y. (2004). Compassion, citizenship and education in South Africa: An opportunity for transformation? *International Review of Education, 50,* 525–543.

Williams, J. H. (2004). Civil conflict, education, and the work of schools: Twelve Propositions. *Conflict Resolution Quarterly, 21,* 471–482.

Yarn, D. H. (2002). Transnational conflict resolution practice: A brief introduction to the context, issues, and search for best practice in exporting conflict resolution. *Conflict Resolution Quarterly, 19,* 303–320.

Diane Bretherton
Jane Weston
Vic Zbar

School-Based Peace Building in Sierra Leone

This article describes the development of a peace education project, including the Peace Education Kit, in schools in Sierra Leone. The program, initiated by the World Bank, has involved working partnerships between local and international agencies and provides a case study of how schools can work with the community to contribute to a national peace-building effort. The project is based in peace theory and the materials developed are integrated into the school curriculum. The approach taken is one of capacity building—working with teachers, workers from nongovernment organizations (NGOs), and mentors. Some of the issues that affect peace education in a postconflict situation, including trauma and religion, are discussed.

Diane Bretherton is the Director of the International Conflict Resolution Centre at the University of Melbourne. Jane Weston is the Senior Project Manager at the Curriculum Corporation. Vic Zbar is an Education Consultant and writer.
Correspondence should be addressed to Diane Bretherton, International Conflict Resolution Centre, The University of Melbourne, Parkville, VIC 3010, Australia. E-mail: dbret@unimelb.edu.au

I was ordered to kill an old woman. When I refused I was tied up and beaten. They threatened to shoot me instead. Then I did something to her. (Saidu, 11 years cited in Pesonen, 2002)

We had peace and then we had war and, God willing, we will have peace again. (Participant in first Sierra Leone *Peace Education Kit* workshop, January 2002)

I use lots of drama and dance because the children really enjoy it. I also use physical games and sports, in part to get the children to accept defeat as much as victory. One they have really enjoyed is the tug of peace rather than tug of war. (Teacher from Bombali District, Sierra Leone, on using the *Peace Education Kit*, March 2005)

SITUATED IN WESTERN AFRICA, Sierra Leone comes up on a number of indexes as the most disadvantaged of nations. The United Nations Human Development Report 2004 noted that Sierra Leone was the lowest ranked of 177 nations surveyed, including having the third-lowest per capita gross domestic product and life expectancy, and having the highest infant mortality rate.

Sierra Leone was a British colony until independence in 1961. The languages spoken are English and Krio, a creole admixture of English, pidgin, and indigenous African. The number of Muslims and Christians in the population is equally divided and a number of animistic indigenous beliefs still hold sway. Though the people are extremely poor, Sierra Leone is a source of valuable diamonds.

In 1991, the Revolutionary United Front (RUF) began attacks against the government and kidnapping, brutality, and terrorism were used to force young people into the armed struggle. A hallmark of the RUF's tactics was the use of amputation—when President Kabbah called for the people to join hands for peace, the RUF delivered bundles of cut-off hands to the steps of parliament house. The war finally ceased in 2000, thanks to UN intervention. Postconflict Sierra Leone is characterized by loss of life, displacement, trauma, and severely damaged government infrastructure. More than 20,000 lives have been lost as a direct result of the conflict, and the United Nations High Commissioner for Refugees (UNHCR) estimates that more than 500,000 people (10% of the population) are refugees, asylum seekers, or internally displaced people (World Bank, 2002, p. 9).

The international aid community has responded with the provision of technical expertise across a range of social domains. In education, over 80% of all schools in Sierra Leone are managed by nongovernmental organizations (NGOs). Organizations such as UNICEF, Plan Sierra Leone, the Norwegian Refugee Council, and others have implemented nonformal primary education programs since 1992, and in some instances since prior to the war (World Bank, 2002). The capacity of the Sierra Leone Ministry of Education, Science, and Technology (MOEST) and others to monitor and coordinate the delivery of these education services has been severely compromised by the war and resulting loss of communications and infrastructure.

"Violence affects schools at multiple levels; attacking individuals, communities and systems and weakening their sense of agency" (Williams, 2004, p. 471). Some of the main education issues for Sierra Leone include the destruction of the school system; the trauma suffered by children and the wider community; the need to reintegrate former combatants, who are themselves children; and the challenge of understanding the past and rebuilding a secure society.

Peace Building

Following the views of peace theorists such as Boulding (1996) and Galtung (1996), the UN promotes a holistic view of peace as more than simply an absence of war. The idea of a culture of peace introduces the notion of shared values linking its member nations and the diverse peoples of the world. It is not so much a peace that is kept by authorities using force, but a peace that is created or built by civil society working in partnership with institutions of the state.

Within this broad view of peace, three main approaches can be discerned. Peacekeeping involves deploying armed forces to ensure there is an absence of hostilities. Peacemaking entails ensuring the cessation of hostilities and the implementation of peace accords. Peacemaking is signaled by the resumption, in the short term, of everyday life—the reopening of schools and shops, the restoration of transport services, and the existence of work opportunities. However, in the long term, to simply rebuild a war-torn society is not enough. A commitment to laying down the foundations for a more peaceful society and removing the policies and practices that led to the war in the first place is known as peace building. This approach needs not only buildings but also builders, hence the current commitment in the international community to capacity building and peace education in postconflict societies.

The *Sierra Leone Peace Education Kit* Project

Peace education can be defined as

the process of promoting the knowledge, skills, attitudes and values needed to bring about behavior changes that will enable children, youth, and adults to prevent conflict and violence, both overt and structural; to resolve conflict peacefully; and to create the conditions conducive to peace whether at an intrapersonal, interpersonal, inter-group, national or international level. (Fountain, 1999, p. 6)

Peace pedagogy emphasizes the role of the peace educator as one who works with students to develop a more positive and elaborate concept of peace, leading them from the most obvious manifestation, the absence of war, through an appreciation of less-visible forms of violence—such as structural inequalities—towards an understanding of the conditions which build positive peace.

Young people played an important role, as combatants and as victims, in the civil conflict in Sierra Leone. As part of its Rehabilitation of Basic Education project, the World Bank decided to ensure that peace education was included in the new curriculum. Though there were already other peace education resources available, most notably the UNHCR's excellent Peace Education Programme kit (2000), none had been developed to specifically address the issues relevant to Sierra Leone.

In 2001, the Bank contracted Curriculum Corporation, a leading Australian education publisher and project management company, to assist them in this goal. Curriculum Corporation's task was initially to develop peace education teaching materials that could be delivered by teachers across a range of school subject areas from years 1 to 9. This was followed in 2003 by an implementation and evaluation program, supported by a World Bank Post-Conflict Fund grant. The project staff include the project manager, Jane Weston, Curriculum Corporation; peace education consultant, Diane Bretherton, University of Melbourne; and education writer and consultant, Vic Zbar. In the first stage of the project, MOEST provided local support; in the second stage, staff from Plan Sierra Leone provided training and assistance to local teachers, as well as other organizational support for the project.

Developing the Curriculum

The first step in the program was to gather information about the various peace education materials and approaches being used in Sierra Leone. Weston and Bretherton traveled to Freetown in January 2002 to meet with MOEST and subsequently plan and conduct a 3-day workshop with more than 50 participants from formal and nonformal education settings. It was clear from the workshop that there were admirable examples of best practice that could provide a starting point for a wider and more systematic peace education program in schools. Participants provided the consultants with copies of materials being used in a variety of formal and nonformal education settings in Sierra Leone. They also alerted the consultants to a range of relevant education and community issues including poverty, trauma, fear, dislocation, and problems associated with the return of excombatants and victims (sometimes amputees) to communities. In addition, approximately 50% of the children in Sierra Leone were not attending school, 50% of teachers were not trained or qualified, and there was a serious shortage of current curriculum materials.

The instructions from the stakeholders were clear. The materials should be inclusive of local input and cultural content, be able to stand alone and be integrated into the Sierra Leone syllabus, flexible and suitable for use in nonformal as well as school settings, be sensitive to Krio and indigenous languages, be written for community workers as well as teachers, be owned by the stakeholders, and have student activities integrated into teacher training modules. Any names, traditions, and so on that were to be included needed to be drawn from Sierra Leone and not other countries or regions, whether African or not.

Back in Australia, the three consultants met to work out a framework to ensure consistency of approach and content. Using this framework, Zbar, assisted by three Australian subject area specialists, wrote the first draft of the Sierra Leone *Peace Education Kit*. A secure consultation Web site was created to allow colleagues in Sierra Leone to view the materials as they were developed. A Sierra Leone-based project officer was contracted to undertake an initial feedback workshop prior to the consultants returning to Freetown to further refine the kit.

The kit consists of four main sections. The introduction sets out the philosophy of peace education. Second, a set of cross-curriculum units covers broad issues teachers may need to take up in their efforts to strengthen peace in Sierra Leone. Third, curriculum units are divided into the areas of English, social studies, health and physical education, and the arts, for students in years 1–2, 3–4, 5–6, 7–8, and 9. Finally, there are whole-school and community activities designed to build a more peaceful school and community in general. Each of the lessons provided in the kit includes specific advice on time required; objectives of the lesson; how teachers should prepare to teach it; required resources, such as chalk or a story to read; the way the lesson should be introduced; instruction on how to teach the lesson and things that students might do; how to end the lesson; suggested further activities for students; assessments that might be useful; and other lessons or activities that teachers might want to do next.

In June 2002, Weston and Zbar returned to Freetown with a complete set of draft materials. A second 2-day workshop brought together a group drawn from the initial consultation and teacher training institutions across the country. As well as collecting feedback on the materials, the aim of this workshop was to model some of the values-clarification activities underpinning the kit and elicit from participants how they might use the materials in their various domains and roles. For example, teacher training colleges might plan to use the materials in their preservice teacher training courses, the MOEST might implement the kit in the context of broader teacher training initiatives, and teachers might plan how to use the materials at the school or faculty level. At the conclusion of this visit, it was clear that the material, after some amendment, would be a useful resource in a range of educational settings.

Working With Teachers

The implementation phase focused on building the capacity of teachers to use the kit for peace building. Our approach to peace education emphasizes process as well as content and the primary and active role played by teachers. The pedagogy—the way in which peace education is done—is as important as the material that is taught.

Schools can teach a great deal about peace and conflict through their approach to knowing. Tidwell (2004) pointed out that children learn very different lessons when knowledge is presented as fixed, authoritative, and unquestionable, as compared to presenting knowledge as interpreted and interpretable, inquiry-based, democratic, and critical. Our aim was to move the educational approach from what Freire (1993) called the banking theory of education, where deposits of knowledge were placed in learners' heads, to a more dynamic education that raises critical consciousness.

The *Peace Education Kit* promotes a variety of alternatives to the use of violence in resolving conflict and places strong emphasis on the use of child-centered pedagogy, offering teachers fresh insights into participative methodologies. Importantly, the kit combines pedagogy with curriculum content, creating a teacher resource that is easy to use and written in plain language. The consultative process ensured that the materials conformed with the Sierra Leone curriculum and were culturally sensitive and appropriate.

Working in partnership with Curriculum Corporation in Australia, Plan Sierra Leone selected 15 mentors who could train teachers in the use of the kit and also support and monitor the teachers' subsequent work in classrooms. In October 2003, Weston and Zbar went to Sierra Leone and conducted a training program for these mentors. Only nine mentors were actually required for the program, but the others acted as backups. The nine mentors were then to assigned one of three regions within one of three districts—Moyamba, Kailahun, and Bombali—where they distributed copies of the *Peace Education Kit* and conducted teacher training. Altogether the mentors reached 90 schools, 900 classroom teachers, and an estimated 4,000 children. Sixty percent of the selected schools were located in urban locations, with the remainder in rural locations. To allow assessment of the impact of the project, 15 comparison schools (receiving no mentor support or input) were chosen in the same districts. Every effort was made to match key variables between the target schools and the comparison schools, including geographic location, total enrollment, gender divisions, and socioeconomic standing.

The training was designed to improve overall classroom teaching skills and help students and teachers build peaceful environments. It was also an essential means to deliver the kit directly to the teachers, as infrastructural difficulties might otherwise have delayed or prevented teachers from obtaining copies of the materials.

Following the training, the mentors have been observing teachers and holding postobservation conferences that encourage teachers to reflect on their current methodologies and uncover ways to improve their skills. Mentors are also providing guidance on the use of various resources described in the kit to make the lessons more effective and suggesting ways to make the overall school climate more conducive for teaching and learning. In addition, mentors are monitoring the use of skills in responding to disciplinary issues and how they are addressed. Mentors repeatedly stress that peace education is not merely a typical classroom subject, but an approach that results in a child-friendly environment that promotes psychosocial adjustment. Monitored behaviors, for example, showing the elimination of corporal punishment by teachers, or an increased ability of students to raise questions in class, are indicative of healthy psychological and social adjustments.

The mentors are looking for a range of key observation points identified in their initial training, such as peace-building initiatives at the school level, that produce an impact in the surrounding school communities. They are taking note of the skills gained by teachers and students participating in the program, focusing on the number and variety of learner-centered teaching methods used in relation to ideas introduced by the kit, the use of outside resources, the development of aids by teachers that enhance principles supported by the kit and the training, and the ability of students to formulate and articulate questions during the presentation of lessons.

Evaluation

The program uses an action research methodology, which involves cycles of planning, implementing, observing, and evaluating at each phase of the project. The cycles of action and reflection are consistent with peace education and allow for constant checking back with partners. The use of this methodology models and reinforces the idea that knowledge is constructed collectively, rather than imposed by a powerful expert.

A baseline survey, developed by Jean Russell of The University of Melbourne on behalf of Curriculum Corporation, was conducted for both sets of schools (those using the kit and those with no intervention) at the outset of the program, with follow-up conducted in January/February 2005. The questionnaires were tested and revised with the help of the mentors during the October 2003 training session to ensure they were culturally appropriate and easy for teachers to complete.

The first survey provided baseline measures of the teachers' sense of efficacy (capacity to make a difference to students' well-being and learning in relation to peace education themes), the degree of implementation by individual teachers of the peace education curriculum and pedagogy (attitudes and actions), and the perceived leadership and school-level support for peace education initiatives. It further measured the perceived impact of peace education teaching and learning on the teachers themselves (e.g., empathic perspective taking, conflict resolution, tolerance, pedagogy), on students (e.g., sense of well being, conflict resolution skills, active learning, attitudes about the future), and on the school culture (e.g., staff modeling of values and skills; staff and student involvement in decision making; perceptions of trust, safety, and respect). In addition, the trial teachers completed questions aimed at evaluating the *Peace Education Kit* training and the usefulness of the kit in their teaching.

When the survey was repeated in early 2005, the data were supplemented with material from a survey of head teachers in trial and comparison schools and qualitative data gathered at workshops and focus groups of teachers, students, and others. At the time of writing this article, the second survey results have not yet been fully evaluated, but are expected to examine broader questions, such as the extent to which the communication skills of teachers and students have improved, the types of techniques employed by teachers and students to resolve issues of conflict without resorting to violence, the range of coping mechanisms that teachers and students have developed for dealing with traumatic events, and types of peace-building initiatives that have emerged at the school and community level.

There is preliminary evidence from focus group meetings conducted in February/March 2005 that indicates that the *Peace Education Kit*, together with the mentor support provided, has contributed significantly toward changing teaching practices, student involvement, and even community attitudes. Of the numerous responses gathered, a representative comment from a teacher in Bombali district was that

> We had problems with the treatment of trauma children, and the kit's stories and activities are helping us to manage these. Conflict resolution activities also have been important because pupils are now resolving more disputes amongst themselves, without resort to violence.

A Kailahun chief also commented that

> Something like this kit is much needed in a community like ours, where it helps to create a more lively community. Seeing peace education being brought here in such a worked-out way is very important, and giving people the tools to work with is already having a positive effect.

Indeed, the most consistent message of the meetings was that demand for the kit exceeded supply, with teachers in nontrial schools wanting to obtain copies.

Capacity-Building Approach

Our definition of peace education includes working at the intrapersonal, interpersonal, intergroup, national, or international levels. Theoretically, we see these levels as nested within one another in an ecological framework (Bronfenbrenner, 1979) so that events within one system will have repercussions at the other levels. The *Peace Education Kit* project methodology is also grounded in ideas derived from "structuration" theory as described by Jabri (1996), who suggested the relationship between the structure of a system and the agency of the actors is complex and the process of transformation is a duet. The systems have a tendency to reproduce themselves, but actors have some power to change their circumstances. Some outcomes can be predicted, but there is also the possibility of unforeseen effects, suggesting the need to monitor interventions for unintended as well as intended effects.

These theoretical ideas suggest that, rather than attempting to bring about change by working against existing systems, an intervention should work with the people and systems that are in place. This approach should enhance their capacity to shape their own lives and environment within the framework provided by the values of a culture of peace.

Features of the Capacity-Building Approach

The capacity-building approach used in the project is evident at a number of levels and coordinates a top-down and bottom-up approach to peace building in schools. At the top level is the sponsorship and direction provided by a global body, the World Bank. At the grassroots level is the direct experiential knowledge of the teachers and NGO workers that was acknowledged and drawn on in the development of the kit. This knowledge was also enhanced by the workshops, which provided opportunities to meet with other workers, discuss issues with international experts, and have access to well-written and systematic materials based on their pooled experience.

Another feature of the capacity-building approach is the cooperation of formal and informal education agencies. A common criticism of education kits is that they sit unused on shelves, but the *Peace Education Kit* has been used widely and appears to be in high demand. This could be attributed, at least in part, to the cooperation of the NGO sector and the MOEST in the development and distribution of the materials. The kit was structured to be an integral part of the MOEST school curriculum, and with the MOEST name on the cover, teachers are more willing to take up the materials.

Another important feature of the capacity-building approach is cooperation across cultures. There was initially some resistance, even incredulity, on the part of the first workshop participants when they met Bretherton and Weston, the two Australian women consultants. It was not long, however, before the participants found themselves engrossed in stories from Bretherton of the struggles and peace-building efforts of people like themselves in distant parts of the world. If local activists, cut off from communication by conflict, can find the opportunity to look at a broader picture, it can lift their feeling of burden and remind them that they are not alone.

Boyden (2003) noted that, in Sierra Leone, rebels employed the strategy of forcing children to commit atrocities to alienate them from their families and communities. This raised the question of the extent to which we need to talk about and understand the past before we can move beyond it. On the one hand, it is accepted practice in the aftermath of conflict to work to some degree with trauma in a psychosocial program. For example, Fuertes (2004, p. 491) stated, "I believe that trauma healing is a vital component of any peace and community building process." On the other hand, a number of those participating in our workshops wanted to omit any reference to trauma from the classroom altogether for fear of causing more hurt and conflict among students. In a situation where all the children were victims of the poverty, educational chaos, lack of security caused by the war, and many bear terrible physical scars, it seemed to the consultants to be unrealistic to pretend that nothing is the matter. In the context of working together across cultural boundaries, this raised the question of who was to make the final decision about this issue. In the end, it was decided to include a carefully written but substantial element on trauma, with an indirect approach, using stories about the experiences of other people, and acknowledgment that teachers as well as students had been exposed to trauma.

Religion and Peace

One of the most interesting aspects of peace education in Sierra Leone concerns the role played by religion. There is a high degree of tolerance and cooperation between Christians and Muslims. It is commonplace to say the Lord's prayer in English and a Muslim prayer in Arabic at the start of meetings, and many individuals participate in both devotions with equal familiarity and comfort. The mutual respect and cooperation that exist between Sierra Leone's Christian and Muslim populations is a fine example to other parts of the world.

The strong hold of religion was evident in the workshops we conducted. The curriculum materials, stories, and picture books collected as examples of local use carried the imprint and discourse of earlier missionary endeavors. Even quite shy participants could present their ideas with resounding strength, as if from a pulpit. This provided a strong value base from which to work, but with a more problematic side for us as peace educators. As the quote from a workshop participant that introduces this article shows, peace is conceived of as something that God bestows, which removes a sense of human agency.

We are not the first to comment on this. The first report of the Secretary General of United Nations Mission to Sierra Leone in 1999 called for a change in reasoning methods. It seemed to him that there was a lack of linkage between criminal acts and repercussions, with a detachment of consequences from the human actions that gave rise to them. To what extent this is a cause, and to what extent it is a result of disempowerment by overwhelming social, political, and economic forces, is not clear.

Conclusion

The development of this project is a continuing story and we are merely at the end of a chapter. Despite the fragile nature of the peace in Sierra Leone, there are some grounds for optimism. The capacity-building approach has worked well to create a productive, cooperative result that is appreciated by the recipients. Rather than peace education being marginal to the curriculum in Sierra Leone, the *Peace Education Kit* is now central to teacher training where it has been introduced. The continuous monitoring and evaluation built into the program will help to further refine the kit and provide more information about the questions we have raised. Should this trial implementation be successful, it is to be hoped that the kit will be distributed more widely and possibly adapted for use in other contexts.

> I just get a feeling of a more peaceful atmosphere in the schools I visit. There is more mingling in the playground, especially among boys and girls who before did not really play together. (Mentor working in Bombali district, Sierra Leone)

References

Boulding, E. (1996). Peace behaviours in various societies. *From a culture of violence to a culture of peace* (pp. 31–54). Peace and Conflict Issues Series. Paris: UNESCO.

Boyden, J. (2003). The moral development of child soldiers: What do adults have to fear? *Peace and Conflict: Journal of Peace Psychology, 9*, 343–362.

Bronfenbrenner, U. (1979). *The ecology of human development: Experiments by nature and by design.* Cambridge, MA: Harvard University Press.

Fountain, S. (1999). *Peace education in UNICEF.* Retrieved May, 2005, from www.unicef.org/programme/education/peace_ed.htm

Freire, P. (1993). *The pedagogy of the oppressed* (M. B. Ramos, Trans.). New York: Continuum.

Fuertes, A. B. (2004). In their own words: Contextualizing the discourse of (war) trauma and healing. *Conflict Resolution Quarterly, 21,* 491–501.

Galtung, J. (1996). Cultural peace: Some characteristics. In *From a culture of violence to a culture of peace* (pp. 75–92). *Peace and conflict issues series.* Paris: UNESCO.

Human Development Report 2004. (2004). New York: United Nations Development Program.

Jabri, V. (1996). *Discourses on violence: Conflict analysis reconsidered.* Manchester, UK: Manchester University Press.

Pesonen, H. (2002). Sierra Leone: Where children draw an end to their Waterloo (Tech. Paper No. 116). In V. Miller & F. W. Affroleter (Eds.), *Helping children outgrow war* (pp. 16–18). Washington, DC: Human Resources and Democracy Division, United States Agency for International Development.

Tidwell, A. (2004). Conflict, peace and education: A tangled web. *Conflict Resolution Quarterly, 21,* 463–470.

United Nations High Commissioner for Refugees. (2000). *Peace education programme.* (Kit) Nairobi, Kenya: Author.

Williams, J. H. (2004). Civil conflict, education and the work of schools: Twelve propositions. *Conflict Resolution Quarterly, 21,* 471–481.

World Bank. (2002). *World Bank: Sierra Leone Rehabilitation of Education Project, Quality Enhancement Review.* Unpublished, Human Development 11, Africa Regional Office, World Bank.

Michael Wessells

Child Soldiers, Peace Education, and Postconflict Reconstruction for Peace

Worldwide, children are drawn into lives as soldiers and terrorism as the result of forced recruitment and also by extremist ideologies and their inability to obtain security, food, power, prestige, education, and positive life options through civilian means. Using an example from Sierra Leone, this article shows that peace education is an essential element in a holistic approach to the reintegration of former child soldiers and to the prevention of youth's engagement in violence and terrorism. In the postconflict context, effective peace education has a stronger practical than didactic focus, and it stimulates empathy, cooperation, reconciliation, and community processes for handling conflict in a nonviolent manner. These processes play a key role also in the prevention of children's engagement in violence and terrorism.

Michael Wessells is a Senior Child Protection Specialist at the Christian Children's Fund and is Professor of Psychology at Randolph-Macon College.
Correspondence should be addressed to Michael Wessells, 17028 Little River Drive, Beaverdam, VA 23015. E-mail: mgwessells@ccfusa.org

A STRIKING, IF SELDOM NOTICED, feature of contemporary armed conflicts is that many of the soldiers are children, defined under international law as people under 18 years of age. Globally, an estimated 300,000 children serve not only as combatants but also as medics, laborers, cooks, domestics, bodyguards, spies, and sex slaves (Brett & McCallin, 1996; Machel, 2001; Singer, 2005; Wessells, 1997). In the post-2002 fighting in Liberia, children comprised nearly half the soldiers (Human Rights Watch, 2004). In Sierra Leone, where the war ended in 2001, nearly half the Revolutionary United Front (RUF) soldiers were children, of whom 25% were girls (McKay & Mazurana, 2004). In Colombia, children make up nearly half of some guerrilla units (Coalition to Stop the Use of Child Soldiers [CSC], 2004). As recently as 2 years ago, the Burmese government forces exploited an estimated 50,000 children as soldiers. Children are exploited as soldiers because, in war zones, children are readily available, cheap, and useful to troop-hungry commanders, who cloak their abuse of children. Commanders frequently prefer child soldiers because they can be manipulated and terrorized and are often willing to accept the most dangerous assignments because they lack a full sense of their own mortality. Worldwide, there are over 500 million lightweight weapons such as the AK-47 assault rifle that enables even 10-year-olds to be effective combatants (Renner, 1999).

This article has two complementary purposes, the first of which is to explain why children become involved in soldiering and the second to provide direction for reintegrating child soldiers back into society. An understanding of why youth join armed groups is necessary for the construction of well-informed means of preventing their engagement as soldiers. In the postconflict environment, a high priority is to reintegrate former child soldiers into civilian society, reducing their propensity to use violence as a means of meeting their needs and continuing cycles of violence. Using reconstruction for peace in Sierra Leone as an example, I attempt to show that peace education, defined broadly to include practical and collective components as well as didactic, individually oriented components, is central to the reintegration of former child soldiers and to the reconstruction of war-torn communities for peace.

Why Children Become Soldiers

Forced recruitment is a common means through which children become soldiers. Using a method of press ganging, armed groups sweep through markets and other public places, forcing mostly poor and marginalized youth to join their ranks. Abduction, too, is a widely used recruitment method. In Northern Uganda, the so called Lord's Resistance Army (LRA) fights the Ugandan government forces by means of a small, highly mobile army, 75% of which consists of abducted children and youth (Human Rights Watch, 2003). To terrorize villages and break the bonds between the children and the community, the LRA often forces children to kill family members or other villagers at the time of their abduction, making it impossible for the children to go home. Known for its brutality, the LRA uses tactics of isolation, physical beatings, and intimidation to force children into complete obedience. Typically, recruits are forced to participate in killing escapees, and over time they are forced to use guns to attack and loot villages, abducting other children. Although not all armed groups exhibit the raw brutality of the LRA, the use of forced recruitment is visible in conflicts in Sierra Leone, Democratic Republic of Congo, Colombia, and Burma, among many others (CSC, 2004).

Also, many children decide to join armed groups without explicit coercion, although their decisions cannot be regarded as voluntary because they are nearly always bounded by desperation and survival needs (Wessells, 2002). Family considerations frequently loom large in children's decisions to join and exhibit a mixture of push and pull factors (Brett & Specht, 2004). Push factors are visible in youth's decisions to join an armed group as a means of escaping an abusive family situation. Not uncommonly, girls decide to join armed groups to escape forced marriages that they do not want (Keairns, 2002). Extreme push factors arise when children's families have been killed or when they have been separated from parents or customary caretakers who might have provided care and protection. Orphans and separated children frequently decide to join armed groups, as a means of obtaining food, security, and health care. Family level pull factors are visible in children's decisions to join armed groups to be with older siblings, an uncle, or a father. In Afghanistan, where large numbers of youth fought in the ranks of the Northern Alliance against the Taliban, many youth joined armed groups in part to be with family members. Also, youth often join armed groups in hopes of earning money that they can send home to support their families.

Desire for revenge also leads youth to join armed groups. As a Philippines youth said, "I joined the movement to avenge my father's death in the hands of the military. When I was seven years old, I saw the military take away my defenseless father from our house" (UNICEF, 2003, p. 28). Psychologically, the desire for revenge justifies killing as a form of retribution. Revenge motives frequently go hand in hand with cognitive images of the people who had committed the wrongdoing as evil, savage, even demonic, figures. By dehumanizing the adversary, such enemy images carve the world into good and evil, exclude the adversary from the moral universe, and absolve one of responsibility for killing and atrocities (White, 1984). Even atrocities and acts of terrorism may seem justified to people who harbor extreme enemy images.

Power, glamour, and excitement also figure in children's decisions to join armed groups (UNICEF, 2003). For youth who have grown up in abject poverty and who have been attacked and have felt powerless, the gun and the military uniform confer a measure of power and prestige that they could not have obtained through other means. The excitement of wielding a gun and participating in military activities offers a stark contrast with the boredom and lack of opportunities youth experience in quiet, rural villages. As a Pakistani boy who had joined the Taliban said, "I enjoyed the task of patrolling Kabul in a latest model jeep, with a Kalashnikov slung over my shoulder. It was a great adventure and made me feel big" (Laeeq & Jawadullah, 2002, p. 7). The excitement offered by military life is a strong incentive for youth who are at a stage in their lives at which risk taking is normal and encouraged by peers.

Children also join armed groups out of disaffection with a political, social, and economic system that has failed them. Lack of educational opportunities, which children see as necessary for building a positive future, is one of the main sources of alienation. In Sierra Leone, youth cited lack of access to education as the primary reason why they had joined the RUF, which promised and offered training that government had failed to provide (Richards, 1996). The paucity of jobs in most war zones, many of which feature unemployment rates as high as 80%, also corrodes youths' sense of hope. Lacking education, jobs, and a sense of hope, and living deeper and deeper in poverty, many youth in war zones spend long hours idling on the streets, where they become easy prey for recruiters who make inflated promises about a better life through joining the armed group.

Ideology and political socialization exert strong influence over youths' decisions to join armed groups. In many countries, opposition groups recruit successfully by playing on youth's sense of victimization, social injustice, and disaffection, as well as their sense of idealism and commitment to their religion. As part of the struggle, oppressed people construct ideologies—societally shared belief systems—that justify the use of violence as an instrument for achieving liberation and political goals that are unattainable through peaceful means. In such societies, poverty and deprivation may be less potent motives than the beliefs and ideas of oppression and liberation that form part of the socialization process for even middle class children. In many societies at war, adults and youth alike use propaganda as a means of motivating youth to join the struggle. During the Taliban era in Afghanistan, for example, adults used religious schools, *madrassahs*, to teach youth to hate and fear outsiders such as the United States. Following 9/11, when U.S. forces attacked the Taliban, youth who had been indoctrinated in the madrassahs in Pakistan swelled the ranks of the Taliban (Rashid, 2000).

For young people who adhere to powerful ideologies, terrorism is a natural extension of their participation in armed conflict. In Sierra Leone, Small Boys Units participated in mutilations wherein the RUF cut off villagers' arms and hands as a means of terrorizing and controlling villages. Many people, young or old, become terrorists because they believe that terrorist activity is their highest commitment to their religion or cause of liberation, and is necessary to overcome evil, win eternal salvation, and defeat the dehumanized Other (Bandura, 2004). In Sri Lanka, for example, the Liberation Tigers of Tamil Eelam (LTTE) selects girls who show strong motivation and the ability to blend in to be suicide bombers. Girls who martyr themselves receive a Heroes Welcome, which is celebrated by the community and confers great prestige on the girls' family (Keairns, 2002). In Palestine, Hamas proclaims youth suicide bombers are martyrs and celebrates their actions in ways that win the family enormous respect (Singer, 2005). Although it has often been suggested that terrorists, whether youth or adults, are mentally ill or deranged, little or no evidence supports this view (McCauley, 2002).

As these examples and many others illustrate, youth are not passive pawns in armed conflict but are actors who find meaning and identity in what they see as the struggle for justice. If finding meaning in life is a powerful incentive for everyone, it is a particularly strong motive for teenagers, who are at a stage in their lives when they are trying out different identities and deciding on their role and place in society (Erikson, 1968). Particularly in situations of social injustice, humiliation, powerlessness, and hopelessness toward the future, extremist ideologies exert a strong grip on young people because they awaken youthful idealism regarding a better life and they answer youths' overarching questions of identity and direction in life.

The Reintegration of Former Child Soldiers

Following armed conflict, a high priority is to reintegrate former child soldiers into civilian life, enabling them to find meaning and positive roles as civilians rather than fighters. Reintegration is a long complex process that is as much about helping children find an appropriate social place as it is about individual rehabilitation, although that, too, is important. Typically, reintegration programs include four key elements. First is family tracing and reintegration efforts that identify the location of children's families, reunite children with their families, and support the families in handling challenges that arise. Second is psychosocial support that helps children come to terms with their war experiences and helps to reconcile the returning children with their communities. Third is livelihood support that includes training in vocational and life skills that enable youth to obtain and hold jobs and also small loans that help them to earn an income. Fourth is education or literacy, which children frequently see as essential for building a positive future.

In many field settings, peace education is woven into reintegration programs, although it is frequently not identified explicitly. Reflecting a distinction found in the literature on peace education, reintegration programs involve teaching *for* peace rather than teaching *about* peace (Brocke-Utne, 1985; Hamburg & Hamburg, 2004; Salomon, 2002). Although former child soldiers may receive an orientation to the peace process when they have been demobilized from armed groups, the emphasis in most reintegration programs is highly practical rather than didactic. Particularly in situations of ongoing ethnic tension or recent intrastate war, the emphasis is frequently on empathy, reconciliation, building the skills and values of nonviolence, and the construction of narratives of living together in harmony. These offer powerful means of breaking through the enemy imaging, extremist ideologies, and social divisions that lead many children to fight.

These practical aspects of peace education are best illustrated by an example from Sierra Leone, where the conflict ended officially in January 2002. At that time, people in rural villages frequently said they felt unconnected to the peace process, saying "What peace? We were hungry before the war, during the war, and still now we are hungry." Building peace was a daunting task because much of the country lay in ruins, people struggled to meet basic needs, and large numbers of soldiers, including children, carried weapons. A 17-year-old who had fought in the RUF told me, "This gun gives me power, and I know how to get what I need. Why should I go back to the village when I have no money and no job, no education?" To address these issues, a national program of disarmament, demobilization, and reintegration was constructed, and UNICEF and international nongovernmental organizations organized the reintegration of former child soldiers. In the Northern Province, which had been the home of the RUF toward the end of the war, girl and boy soldiers were returning home to the villages they had attacked and local villagers typically feared them or sought revenge. Former child soldiers were frequently stigmatized as rebels, and girls who had been raped and who had become mothers were harassed or regarded as if they were damaged goods (Kostelny, 2004).

To aid the reintegration of child soldiers and also young adult soldiers, Christian Children's Fund (CCF) used a holistic, community empowerment approach that included the customary element sketched earlier (Wessells & Jonah, in press). However, education for peace was interwoven into the project by virtue of the way in which it was implemented. In particular, the project made extensive use of the principle that cooperation on shared goals is an effective means of reducing tension and improving intergroup relations (Johnson & Johnson, 1989; Sherif et al., 1961). It also built on the value of empathy and traditional reconciliation processes in reducing conflict and on community service as a means of helping former child soldiers achieve a positive social role.

In the first phase of the project, each of 15 communities held open meetings to discuss the end of the war, what it meant for villagers, concerns about children's well-being, and how to move forward. These discussions, which helped people to take a positive future orientation, frequently identified villages' needs for schools or health posts that had been damaged or destroyed during the war. CCF's Sierra Leonen staff helped to facilitate discussions in which the communities prioritized these needs and selected a project such as building a school that would benefit children. Issues of child soldiers and reconciliation were delicately woven into these discussions. Because most villagers had viewed child soldiers as attackers who had not suffered, the CCF staff led dialogues on how children had become soldiers. These dialogues emphasized that suffering had led children to enter armed groups and showed also how children had suffered as soldiers. With empathy having opened the door for reconciliation, the CCF staff stimulated reflection on how to live together as one people. Villagers responded enthusiastically because they were very tired of war and knew that people from the same villages had fought against each other. Awakening older forms of nonviolent conflict resolution, villagers spontaneously offered proverbs, songs, or dances that evoked themes of unity, forgiveness, and reconciliation.

In the next stage, the village youth built the project—typically a school or health post—that the community had prioritized. As youth worked, they earned a small stipend, which was crucial because many former youth soldiers said that without an income they would have returned to the bush to fight again. The building was a cooperative endeavor by former child soldiers and village youth, who said they learned in the process to see each other as human and approachable. This activity transformed villagers' attitudes toward the former child soldiers, whom they now saw as people who had much to contribute to the community. Also, the physical construction had a powerful effect, as many villagers said that they experienced increased hope because they now saw tangible signs of progress and venues for supporting their children.

As the building continued, additional dialogues probed the possibilities for reconciliation. One chief told of a local method for rehabilitating former child soldiers who had shared their story with their parents. First, the parents approached the chief and asked him to speak with their child. If the chief agreed, he met with the child, who prostrated himself before the chief and held his ankle as gestures of submission, and then told his story. If the chief believed he was truthful and remorseful, he assigned the child to an adult for moral tutelage and guidance in community service. Like the cooperative work project, this community service approach was a matter of peace education through praxis. For the girls who had been violated and were seen as spiritually polluted, local healers performed cleaning rituals believed to remove the spiritual impurities and restore harmony with the ancestors (Kostelny, 2004). These rituals were important because in many sub-Saharan countries, local people view spiritual contamination as the major barrier to a child soldier's reconciliation with the community (Wessells & Monteiro, 2004).

In the third stage, former boy and girl soldiers received training in skills such as carpentry, tailoring, and tie-dyeing that market research had indicated were sources of jobs locally. They learned and worked under the direction of a master artisan who also served as a mentor and moral guide. The youth had frequent discussions about how to handle conflict without recourse to violence, about their role in the community, and about their hope for the future. Because conflicts occurred in the community over issues such as land and women, participants in the village meetings decided to create conflict resolution committees that worked locally to mediate disputes, referred particularly difficult cases to appropriate legal or traditional bodies, and supported local norms of nonviolent conflict resolution.

This project, which has subsequently been expanded into other provinces, enjoyed considerable success, visible in reductions of fighting and increased integration of former child soldiers into their villages. Despite dire predictions that villages would never accept back the youth who had attacked them, over 90% of former child soldiers have gone home and say they now have a civilian identity and hope of a positive life as civilians. Communities, too, say they see the former child soldiers not as troublemakers but as youth who have a spirit of community service.

Although this is only one example, it shows that peace education in a postconflict setting is a collective, practical project that aids the reintegration of former child soldiers by stimulating empathy, cooperation, reconciliation, and community processes for handling conflict in a nonviolent manner. This example is significant in part because it shows that it is possible to break the seemingly iron grip of ideologies of hatred, which the RUF had used to indoctrinate youth fighters. Also, it offers valuable clues about how to prevent youth's engagement in violence and terrorism. The project succeeded in part because it created for former fighters a set of positive life options and skills and values of nonviolence that they had not had before the war. Much youth violence is preventable by creating positive life options and socializing them for peace rather than war. A significant task for peace educators worldwide is to use their practical tools to counter the extremist ideologies and limited life options that draw youth into lives of violence and terrorism.

Although this work was conducted in a war zone, the findings have implications for peace education in school settings in more stable contexts. The tactic of reducing intergroup tensions through collaboration on shared goals applies as much to schools where rival groups or gangs exist as to war-torn communities. Even in schools that are relatively free of fighting and intergroup rivalries, the findings of this study provide a useful launching point for activist and consciousness-raising work by students on addressing global issues of war and peace. One very practical suggestion is for peace educators to work with their students on school and local area campaigns that raise awareness about the problem of child soldiering and steps to address the problem. Through connection with the global Coalition to Stop the Use of Child Soldiers, students can become effective advocates for healthier policies that protect children's rights and well-being. The need for this kind of work is indicated most clearly by the fact that the United States is one of only two members of the UN that has not ratified the Convention on the Rights of the Child, which outlaws child soldiering. That the other country that has not ratified the Convention is Somalia speaks volumes about the challenges that lie ahead.

References

Bandura, A. (2004). The role of selective moral disengagement in terrorism and counterterrorism. In F. Moghaddam & A. Marsella (Eds.), *Understanding terrorism: Psychosocial roots, consequences, and interventions* (pp. 121–150). Washington, DC: American Psychological Association.

Brett, R., & McCallin, M. (1996). *Children: The invisible soldiers*. Vaxjo, Sweden: Radda Barnen.

Brett, R., & Specht, I. (2004). *Young soldiers: Why they choose to fight*. Boulder, CO: Lynne Rienner.

Brocke-Utne, B. (1985). *Educating for peace: A feminist perspective*. New York: Pergamon.

Coalition to Stop the Use of Child Soldiers. (2004). *Child soldiers global report 2004*. London: Author.

Erikson, E. (1968). *Identity, youth, and crisis*. New York: Norton.

Hamburg, D., & Hamburg, B. (2004). *Learning to live together: Preventing hatred and violence in child and adolescent development*. New York: Oxford University Press.

Honwana, A. (1997). Healing for peace: Traditional healers and post-war reconstruction in Southern Mozambique. *Peace and Conflict: Journal of Peace Psychology, 3,* 293–305.

Human Rights Watch. (2003). *Stolen children: Abduction and recruitment in Northern Uganda*. New York: Author.

Human Rights Watch. (2004). *How to fight, how to kill: Child soldiers in Liberia*. New York: Author.

Johnson, D., & Johnson, R. (1989). *Cooperation and competition: Theory and research*. Edina, MN: Interaction.

Keairns, Y. (2002). *The voices of girl child soldiers: Summary*. New York: Quaker United Nations Office.

Kostelny, K. (2004). What about the girls? *Cornell International Law Journal, 37,* 505–512.

Laeeq, A., & Jawadullah, M. (2002). Flowers on the frontline. *Child Soldiers Newsletter, 5,* 6–7.

Machel, G. (2001). *The impact of war on children.* Cape Town, South Africa: David Philip.

McCauley, C. (2002). Psychological issues in understanding terrorism and the response to terrorism. In C. Stout (Ed.), *The psychology of terrorism.* Vol. III. Theoretical understandings and perspectives (pp. 3–29). Westport, CT: Praeger.

McKay, S., & Mazurana, D. (2004). *Where are the girls? Girls in fighting forces in Northern Uganda, Sierra Leone, and Mozambique: Their lives during and after war.* Montreal, Canada: International Centre for Human Rights and Democratic Development.

Rashid, A. (2000). *Taliban.* New Haven, CT: Yale University Press.

Renner, M. (1999). Arms control orphans. *The Bulletin of the Atomic Scientists, 55*(1), 22–26.

Richards, P. (1996). *Fighting for the rain forest: War, youth & resources in Sierra Leone.* Oxford, UK: International Africa Institute.

Salomon, G. (2002). The nature of peace education: Not all programs are created equal. In G. Salomon & B. Nevo (Eds.), *Peace education: The concept, principles, and practices around the world* (pp. 33–13). Mahwah, NJ: Lawrence Erlbaum Associates, Inc.

Sherif, M., Harvey, O., White, B., Hood, W., & Sherif, C. (1961). *Intergroup cooperation and competition: The Robbers Cave experiment.* Norman, OK: University Book Exchange.

Singer, P. (2005). *Children at war.* New York: Pantheon.

UNICEF. (2003). *Adult wars, child soldiers: Voices of children involved in armed conflict in the East Asia and Pacific Region.* Bangkok, Thailand: Author.

Wessells, M. G. (1997). Child soldiers. *Bulletin of the Atomic Scientists, 53*(6), 32–39.

Wessells, M. (2002). Recruitment of children as soldiers in sub-Saharan Africa: An ecological analysis. In L. Mjoset & S. Van Holde (Eds.), *The comparative study of conscription in the armed forces* (Comparative Social Research, Vol. 20; pp. 237–254). Amsterdam, The Netherlands: Elsevier.

Wessells, M. G., & Jonah, D. (in press). Reintegration of former youth soldiers in Sierra Leone: Challenges of reconciliation and post-accord peacebuilding. In S. McEvoy (Ed.), *Youth and post-accord peacebuilding.* South Bend, IN: University of Notre Dame Press.

Wessells, M. G., & Monteiro, C. (2004). Healing the wounds following protracted conflict in Angola: A community-based approach to assisting war-affected children. In U. P. Gielen, J. Fish, & J. G. Draguns (Eds.), *Handbook of culture, therapy, and healing* (pp. 321–341). Mahwah, NJ: Lawrence Erlbaum Associates, Inc.

White, R. (1984). *Fearful warriors: A psychological profile of U.S.-Soviet relations.* New York: Free Press.

Additional Resources for Classroom Use

Johnson and Johnson, Essential Components of Peace Education (pp. 280–292)

1. Cooperative learning center's web site: www.co-operation.org

   This Web site contains recent writings on cooperative learning and descriptions of implementation efforts from around the world. Center's newsletter may be accessed from this site.

2. Johnson, D. W., Johnson, R., & Holubec, E. (1998). *Cooperation in the classroom.* Edina, MN: Interaction Book Company.

   This book provides basic information about the nature of cooperative learning and how to implement in elementary and secondary school classrooms.

3. Johnson, D. W., Johnson, R., & Smith, K. (2006). *Active learning: Cooperation in the college classroom.* Edina, MN: Interaction Book Company.

   This book describes the nature of different types of cooperative learning and how they may be implemented in postsecondary settings.

4. Johnson, D. W., & Johnson, R. (2005). *Teaching students to be peacemakers.* Edina, MN: Interaction Book Company.

   This book describes the nature of the Peacemaker Program and how it may be implemented in elementary and secondary schools.

5. Johnson, D. W., & Johnson, R. (1995). *Creative controversy: Intellectual challenge in the classroom.* Edina, MN: Interaction Book Company.

   This book describes the nature of creative controversy and describes how it may be implemented in elementary, secondary, and postsecondary settings.

Kupermintz and Salomon, Lessons to be Learned From Research on Peace Education in the Context of Intractable Conflict (pp. 293–302)

1. Center for Positive Practices Web Site

   http://www.positivepractices.com/PeaceEducation/PeaceEducationAEAbstracts.html

   An alphabetically organized detailed list of annotated curricula, articles, and peace education resources.

2. Workable Peace Project Web Site

   http://www.workablepeace.org/curriculum.html

   The Workable Peace curriculum integrates the study of intergroup conflict and the development of critical thinking, problem solving, and perspective-taking skills into social studies and humanities content. It helps teachers and students understand and make connections among conflicts around the world, in the United States, and in their own schools and communities. The curriculum provides teachers with an academically rigorous framework and a rich set of materials for teaching about conflict as a major theme in history and current events. Using a unique combination of content and skill activities, it enables students to learn about history in ways that enliven the imagination, awaken moral reasoning, and impart social and civic skills that they can use throughout their lives.

3. Glooscap Elementary School Web Site

http://www.go.ednet.ns.ca/glooscap/peacefulschool/peaceful.html

The Peace Education Curriculum Committee of Glooscap Elementary School has developed a Curriculum Manual on Peace Education and Emotional Literacy. The manual contains materials for teachers to plan and implement a comprehensive program in this curricular area. Teachers may use the resources cited in the manual to complement and supplement their individual classroom programs. Six learning units are offered, dealing with the nature of conflict, feelings, communication, friendship, self-esteem, rights, and responsibilities.

Gassin, Enright, and Knutson, Bringing Peace to the Central City: Forgiveness Education in Milwaukee (pp. 319–328)

1. Knutson, J. A., & Enright, R. D. (2002). *The adventure of forgiveness: A first-grade forgiveness curriculum.* Madison, WI: International Forgiveness Institute. (1127 University Avenue # 201, Madison WI 53715)

   Knutson, J. A., & Enright, R. D. (2003). *Discovering forgiveness: A guided curriculum for second-grade children.* Madison, WI: International Forgiveness Institute. (1127 University Avenue # 201, Madison WI 53715)

   Knutson, J. A., & Enright, R. D. (2004). *The joy of forgiveness: A guided curriculum for third-grade children.* Madison, WI: International Forgiveness Institute. (1127 University Avenue # 201, Madison WI 53715)

   The three forgiveness curriculum guides are available on CD from the International Forgiveness Institute (director@forgiveness-institute.org) for $39.95 each. Please note that each curriculum guide does not include the children's books and DVDs that are part of the forgiveness curriculum. The guides show the teacher about each lesson and how to conduct that lesson, along with questions and proposed activities.

Lodge and Frydenberg, The Role of Peer Bystanders in School Bullying: Positive Steps Towards Promoting Peaceful Schools (pp. 329–336)

1. Espelage, D., & Swearer, S. (Eds.). (2004). *Bullying in American schools: A social-ecological perspective on prevention and intervention.* Mahwah, NJ: Lawrence Erlbaum Associates, Inc.

   The editors of this book have compiled a broad cross section of the current research on bullying and prevention strategies.

2. Rigby, K. (2003). *Stop the Bullying: A handbook for schools.* Melbourne, Australia: ACER.

   This comprehensive handbook contains practical advice for educators and parents who want to know how to stop bullying. It incorporates up-to-date content, including lesson materials for teachers working with students in classrooms, instructional material for school staff in examining and addressing bullying, and advice relating to bullying involving adults in the school community. Also provided are extensive references to current research and accessible resources. Web site: www.education.unisa.edu.au/bullying/

3. Olweus Bullying Prevention Program

   http://www.clemson.edu/olweus/

   The Olweus Bullying Prevention Program is a comprehensive, school-wide program designed for use in elementary, middle, or junior high schools. Its goals are to reduce and prevent bullying problems among school children and to improve peer relations at school.

Niens and Cairns, Conflict, Contact, and Education in Northern Ireland (pp. 337–344)

1. Gallagher, T. (2004). *Education in Divided Societies.* New York: Palgrave Macmillan.

   The book examines the role of education in a number of societies that deal with divisions, such as race (United States, Britain, South Africa), religion (Northern Ireland, Netherlands) and language (Spain, Belgium). It concludes by drawing lessons from the societies' experiences and argues that structures need to be supported by processes of dialogue and interconnected social systems for change to occur.

2. Northern Ireland Council for Integrated Education Web Site

   http://www.nicie.org/

   This key Web site provides an overview of integrated education in Northern Ireland. In addition to listing most up-to-date information about schools and pupils, recent publications relating to integrated education are announced, which can often be downloaded.

3. Transform Conflict Web Site

   http://www.transformconflict.org/

   This site will be of interest to teachers and other educational professionals involved in the development of citizenship education. It will be particularly useful to those interested in developing cross-border and/or transnational links with other schools. The site provides materials and approaches to citizenship and human rights education and it facilitates the establishment of links between schools in Northern Ireland and the Republic of Ireland.

Jones, Implementing Community Peace and Safety Networks in South Africa (pp. 345–354)

1. Harris, I. M., & Morrison, M. L. (2003). *Peace education* (2nd ed.). Jefferson, NC: McFarland & Co.

   This general book on peace education has several sections relevant to statements about the current adequacy of research and evaluation. The authors argue peace education programs have one or more of the following goals: (a) help to appreciate the richness of the concept of peace, (b) address fears, (c) provide information about security, (d) understand war behavior, (e) develop intercultural understanding, (f) provide a *futures* orientation, (g) teach peace as a process, (h) promote a concept of peace accompanied by social justice, (i) stimulate a respect for life, and (j) manage conflicts nonviolently. They classify conflict resolution education as an approach to peace education that helps individuals understand conflict dynamics and empowers them to use communication skills and build and manage peaceful relationships.

2. Nevo, B., & Brem, I. (2002). Peace education programs and the evaluation of their effectiveness. In G. Salomon & B. Nevo (Eds.), *Peace education: The concept, principles, and practices around the world* (pp. 271–282). Mahwah, NJ: Lawrence Erlbaum Associates, Inc.

   These authors have attempted to gather the past 20 years of evaluation research on the effectiveness of a Peace Education program. They note that between 1981 and 2000 approximately 1,000 articles, chapters, reports, and symposia proceedings, dealing with a broadly defined peace education area, were listed on numerous data bases (ERIC, PsychLit, PsychInfo, etc.). Approximately 30% of these sources referred to a specific peace education intervention. They then created a taxonomy to summarize characteristic features of these programs. Of the approximately 300 published pieces on peace education intervention programs, about 100 had some report of effectiveness evaluation, but only 79 had sufficient detail for any analysis (full bibliography of all 79 sources are included as an Appendix in the back of their chapter). This chapter does not evaluate these studies in terms of their facets, but reports a general finding that the majority of these programs (51 out of 79) were found to be partially or highly effective.

3. Smythe, M., & Robinson, G. (Eds.). (2001). *Researching violently divided societies: Ethical and methodological issues*. New York: United Nations University Press.

This edited volume addresses many of the ethical and methodological difficulties of conducting research in violently divided societies. Although it does not focus specifically, or even significantly, on peace education, the concerns are applicable to researching peace education programs implemented in contexts of ongoing and active violence between parties. The book is a product of Initiative on Conflict Resolution and Ethnicity (INCORE), an initiative established by the United Nations University and the University of Ulster. More information on INCORE and its work can be found at www.incore.ulst.ac.uk, and www.incore.ulst.ac.uk/ecrd/ (for specific links to the Ethnic Conflict Research Digest).

Bretherton, Weston, and Zbar, School-Based Peace Building in Sierra Leone (pp. 355–362)

1. *Journal of Peace Education* Web Site

   http://www.tandf.co.uk/journals/titles/17400201.asp

   This relatively new journal, sponsored by the Peace Education Commission, promotes discussions on theories, research, and practices in peace education in varied educational and cultural settings, using a multidisciplinary and intercultural approach.

2. *OJPCR: Online Journal of Peace and Conflict Resolution* Web Site

   http://trinstitute.org/ojpcr/

   A resource for students, teachers, and practitioners in fields relating to the reduction and elimination of destructive conflict.

3. Educators for Social Responsibility Web Site

   http://www.esrnational.org/home.htm

   Includes the Online Teacher Center, which provides teaching resources on a range of issues related to international security, conflict resolution, peacemaking, violence prevention, and social responsibility.

Wessells, Child Soldiers, Peace Education, and Post-Conflict Reconstruction for Peace (pp. 363–369)

1. Coalition to Stop the Use of Child Soldiers Web Site

   www.child-soldiers.org

   This Web site has up to date information from around the world on the use of child soldiers in various countries and also on the prevention and rehabilitation of child soldiers.

2. Human Rights Watch Web Site

   www.hrw.org

   This Web site is one of the best sources of reports and information on the exploitation of children as soldiers.

INDEX TO VOLUME XLIV

Additional Resources for Classroom Use, 72–75, 178–182, 270–273, 370–373.

Applying Gifted Education Pedagogy to Total Talent Development for All Students. Joseph S. Renzulli, 80–89.

Are "Other People's Children" Constructivist Learners Too? Francis Bailey & Ken Pransky, 19–26.

Bailey, Francis, & Pransky, Ken. Are "Other People's Children" Constructivist Learners Too? 19–26.

Baldwin, Alexinia Y. Identification Concerns and Promises for Gifted Students of Diverse Populations, 105–114.

Bretherton, Diane, Weston, Jane & Zbar, Vic. School-Based Peace Building in Sierra Leone, 355–362.

Brimijoin, Kay. Differentiation and High-Stakes Testing: An Oxymoron? 254–261.

Bringing Peace to the Central City: Forgiveness Education in Milwaukee. Elizabeth A. Gassin, Robert D. Enright, & Jeanette A. Knutson, 319–328.

Broderick, Alicia A., Mehta-Parekh, Heeral, & Reid, D. Kim. Differentiating Instruction for Disabled Students in Inclusive Classrooms, 194–202.

Callahan, Carolyn M. Identifying Gifted Students From Underrepresented Populations, 98–104.

Challenges and Possibilities for Serving Gifted Learners in the Regular Classroom. Joyce VanTassel-Baska & Tamra Stambaugh, 211–217.

Child Soldiers, Peace Education, and Postconflict Reconstruction for Peace. Michael Wessells, 363–369.

Conflict, Contact, and Education in Northern Ireland. Ulrike Niens & Ed Cairns, 337–344.

Cultural Diversity, Motivation, and Differentiation. Margery B. Ginsberg, 218–225.

Differentiating Instruction for Disabled Students in Inclusive Classrooms. Alicia A. Broderick, Heeral Mehta-Parekh, & D. Kim Reid, 194–202.

Differentiated Instruction and Educational Standards: Is Détente Possible? Jay McTighe & John L. Brown, 234–244.

Differentiation and High-Stakes Testing: An Oxymoron? Kay Brimijoin, 254–261.

Essential Components of Peace Education. David W. Johnson & Roger T. Johnson, 280–292.

Ford, Donna Y., & Moore, James L. III. This Issue: Gifted Education, 77–79.

Ford, Donna Y., Moore, James L. III, & Harmon, Deborah A. Integrating Multicultural and Gifted Education: A Curricular Framework, 125–137.

From Moral Exclusion to Moral Inclusion: Theory for Teaching Peace. Susan Opotow, Janet Gerson, & Sarah Woodside, 303–318.

Garcia, Juanita, & Donmoyer, Robert. Providing Technical Assistance to Improve Student Performance: Insights From the Collaborative Inquiry Project, 63–71.

Gassin, Elizabeth A., Enright, Robert D., & Knutson, Jeanette A. Bringing Peace to the Central City: Forgiveness Education in Milwaukee, 319–328.

George, Paul S. A Rationale for Differentiating Instruction in the Regular Classroom, 185–193.

Gifted Programs and Services: What Are the Nonnegotiables? Joyce VanTassel-Baska, 90–97.

Ginsberg, Margery B. Cultural Diversity, Motivation, and Differentiation, 218–225.

Grading and Differentiation: Paradox or Good Practice. Carol Ann Tomlinson, 262–269.

Grantham, Tarek C., Frasier, Mary M., Roberts, Angie C., & Bridges, Eric M. Parent Advocacy for Culturally Diverse Gifted Students, 138–147.

Hirsh, Stephanie. Professional Development and Closing the Achievement Gap, 38–44.

Identification and Assessment of Gifted Students With Learning Disabilities. Lilia M. Ruban & Sally M. Reis, 115–124.

Identification Concerns and Promises for Gifted Students of Diverse Populations. Alexinia Y. Baldwin, 105–114.

Identifying Gifted Students From Underrepresented Populations. Carolyn M. Callahan, 98–104.

Implementing Community Peace and Safety Networks in South Africa. Tricia S. Jones, 345–354.

Integrating Multicultural and Gifted Education: A Curricular Framework. Donna Y. Ford, James L. Moore III, & Deborah A. Harmon, 125–137.

Jackson, Yvette. Unlocking the Potential of African American Students: Keys to Reversing Underachievement, 203–210.

Johnson, David W., & Johnson, Roger T. This Issue: Peace Education, 275–279.

Johnson, David W., & Johnson, Roger T. Essential Components of Peace Education, 280–292.

Johnson, Joseph F., Jr. & Uline, Cynthia L. Preparing Educational Leaders to Close Achievement Gaps, 45–52.

Jones, Tricia S. Implementing Community Peace and Safety Networks in South Africa, 345–354.

Kupermintz, Haggai, & Salomon, Gavriel. Lessons to be Learned From Research on Peace Education in the Context of Intractable Conflict, 293–302.

Leaders as Policy Mediators: The Reconceptialization of Accountability. Andrea K. Rorrer & Linda Skrla, 53–62.

Lessons to be Learned From Research on Peace Education in the Context of Intractable Conflict. Haggai Kupermintz & Gavriel Salomon, 293–302.

Lodge, Jodie, & Frydenberg, Erica. The Role of Peer Bystanders in School Bullying: Positive Steps Toward Promoting Peaceful Schools, 329–336.

McClure, Phyllis. Where Standards Come From, 4–10.

McTighe, Jay, & Brown, John L. Differentiated Instruction and Educational Standards: Is Détente Possible? 234–244.

Merging Social Justice and Accountability: Educating Qualified and Effective Teachers. Mary S. Poplin & John Rivera, 27–37.

Moon, Tonya R. The Role of Assessment in Differentiation, 226–233.

Moore, James L. III, Ford, Donna Y., & Milner, H. Richard. Underachievement Among Gifted Students of Color: Implications for Educators, 167–177.

Niens, Ulrike & Cairns, Ed. Conflict, Contact, and Education in Northern Ireland, 337–344.

Opotow, Susan, Gerson, Janet, & Woodside, Sarah. From Moral Exclusion to Moral Inclusion: Theory for Teaching Peace, 303–318.

Parent Advocacy for Culturally Diverse Gifted Students. Tarek C. Grantham, Mary M. Frasier, Angie C. Roberts, & Eric M. Bridges, 138–147.

Poplin, Mary S., & Rivera, John. Merging Social Justice and Accountability: Educating Qualified and Effective Teachers, 27–37.

Preparing Educational Leaders to Close Achievement Gaps. Joseph F. Johnson, Jr., & Cynthia L. Uline, 45–52.

Professional Development and Closing the Achievement Gap. Stephanie Hirsh, 38–44.

Providing Technical Assistance to Improve Student Performance: Insights From the Collaborative Inquiry Project. Juanita Garcia & Robert Donmoyer, 63–71.

Quality Curriculum and Instruction for Highly Able Students. Carol Ann Tomlinson, 160–166.

Rationale for Differentiating Instruction in the Regular Classroom, A. Paul S. George, 185–193.

Reis, Sally M., & Ruban, Lilia M. Services and Programs for Academically Talented Students With Learning Disabilities, 148–159.

Renzulli, Joseph S. Applying Gifted Education Pedagogy to Total Talent Development for All Students, 80–89.

Role of Assessment in Differentiation, The. Tonya R. Moon, 226–233.

Role of Peer Bystanders in School Bullying: Positive Steps Toward Promoting Peaceful Schools, The. Jodie Lodge & Erica Frydenberg, 329–336.

Rorrer, Andrea K., & Skrla, Linda. Leaders as Policy Mediators: The Reconceptualization of Accountability, 53–62.

Ruban, Lilia M., & Reis, Sally M. Identification and Assessment of Gifted Students With Learning Disabilities, 115–124.

Services and Programs for Academically Talented Students With Learning Disabilities. Sally M. Reis & Lilia M. Ruban, 148–159.

School-Based Peace Building in Sierra Leone. Diane Bretherton, Jane Weston, & Vic Zbar, 355–362.

Sternberg, Robert J., & Zhang, Li-fang. Styles of Thinking as a Basis of Differentiated Instruction, 245–253.

Stiggins, Rick, & Chappuis, Jan. Using Student-Involved Classroom Assessment to Close Achievement Gaps, 11–18.

Styles of Thinking as a Basis of Differentiated Instruction. Robert J. Sternberg & Li-fang Zhang, 245–253.

This Issue: Closing Achievement Gaps: What Will It Take? Cynthia L. Uline & Joseph F. Johnson, Jr., 1–3.

This Issue: Differentiated Instruction. Carol Tomlinson, 183–184.

This Issue: Gifted Education. Donna Y. Ford & James L. Moore III, 77–79.

This Issue: Peace Education. David W. Johnson & Roger T. Johnson, 275–279.

Tomlinson, Carol. This Issue: Differentiated Instruction, 183–184.

Tomlinson, Carol Ann. Grading and Differentiation: Paradox or Good Practice, 262–269.

Tomlinson, Carol Ann. Quality Curriculum and Instruction for Highly Able Students, 160–166.

Uline, Cynthia L., & Johnson, Joseph F., Jr. This Issue: Closing Achievement Gaps: What Will It Take? 1–3.

Underachievement Among Gifted Students of Color: Implications for Educators. James L. Moore III, Donna Y. Ford, & H. Richard Milner, 167–177.

Unlocking the Potential of African American Students: Keys to Reversing Underachievement. Yvette Jackson, 203–210.

Using Student-Involved Classroom Assessment to Close Achievement Gaps. Rick Stiggins, & Jan Chappuis, 11–18.

VanTassel-Baska, Joyce. Gifted Programs and Services: What Are the Nonnegotiables? 90–97.

VanTassel-Baska, Joyce, & Stambaugh, Tamra. Challenges and Possibilities for Serving Gifted Learners in the Regular Classroom, 211–217.

Wessells, Michael. Child Soldiers, Peace Education, and Postconflict Reconstruction for Peace, 363–369.

Where Standards Come From. Phyllis McClure, 4–10.